PORTRAIT OF
WILLIAM MORRIS

by
ESTHER MEYNELL

"A rock of defence to us all, and a castle on
the top of it, and a banner on the top of that."
EDWARD BURNE-JONES

"Morris is beaten gold."
JOHN RUSKIN

LONDON
CHAPMAN & HALL
1947

PORTRAIT OF WILLIAM MORRIS

MORRIS IN HIS STUDY AT KELMSCOTT HOUSE.

(Photo: Emery Walker Ltd.)

*This book is produced in complete conformity with
the authorized economy standards*

PRINTED IN GREAT BRITAIN BY JARROLD AND SONS, LTD., NORWICH
BOUND BY G. AND J. KITCAT LTD., LONDON: FLEXIBACK BINDING

CAT. NO. 4107/4

FOR

EDWARD WILLIAM HUNTER

BECAUSE OF OUR LONG FRIENDSHIP

AND REMEMBERING

ELISABETH

CONTENTS

ILLUSTRATIONS

FOREWORD

This book is intended as a study of Morris himself, and not of his work as craftsman or author. These aspects of his life have been considered in detail by competent authorities. So much in detail, in fact, that Morris has been somewhat submerged under the flood of his activities. But one thing emerges, I find, in writing of him: that strong as Morris's personality undoubtedly was—that is shown by the deep impression he made on all who knew him—it is curiously elusive. There was something strange and unexplained about him.

J. W. Mackail's *Life of Morris* still, after nearly fifty years, remains the authoritative biography; and to that must be added the Introductions written for the twenty-four volumes of Morris's *Collected Works*, by his daughter May Morris. They are of the utmost value, being first-hand and authentic. I am indebted to Messrs. Longmans Green, Ltd., and the Society of Antiquaries, for permission to quote from these Introductions. Linked with them is Lady Burne-Jones's *Memorials* of her husband, and to her daughter, Mrs. Mackail, I am grateful for a similar permission. Also to Messrs. Secker and Warburg, Ltd., and to the Executors of Wilfred Scawen Blunt for the same kindness in regard to Blunt's *My Diaries*.

E. M.

1*

PROLOGUE

So much of the work of William Morris was concrete craftsmanship—things which could be seen and handled, wallpapers, printed fabrics, embroideries, tapestries, illuminations, printed books—that a general belief has grown up that he was a simple kind of man, someone strayed out of the Middle Ages, puzzled as a child might be by the complications of a machine-made, industrial civilization. His vigorous and forthright personality, his looks, on which many of his friends commented, like that of a "sea-captain", increased this outward impression of simplicity and directness. A man with such a passion for using his hands, for making things, such an intuitive craftsman and creator as William Morris, is never expected to have a particularly subtle or sensitive mind. Therefore Morris, so skilful and abounding a patternmaker, was himself fitted into a pattern which actually left him little room for growth or development.

There he has more or less stayed for the fifty years since his death in 1896; respected and admired, but a little dated, like his wallpapers and his chintzes. We prefer plain surfaces to-day—we find that luxuriant and rampant vitality of the medieval carvers and painters and weavers a little exhausting.

But here and there in some minds the thought is dawning that there was more to Morris than cretonnes and wallpapers. That he was not simple at all, but very difficult to know—that in the words of one so different from himself:

> . . . you must love him, e'er to you,
> He will seem worthy of your love.

Watts's portrait of Morris, painted when Morris was thirty-six, in the full flood of his maturity and power, emphasizes this. Get past the first somewhat entangling impression of leafy background and luxuriant locks, and look at the face. There is a noble amplitude about it—the spacious forehead, the candid brows, the broad cheeks, as of one who enjoyed life; the slightly feminine and sensitive mouth contradicted by the firm-set chin. But the light and meaning of a face in repose, lies mostly in the eyes, and those eyes are very curious. For one thing they are different in expression—the right eye is alert and forth-looking, the left is dreamy and remote, with a slightly drooped lid. The general impression given by both of them is that the eyes keep a guard on the inner Morris, that they do not reveal but conceal. He is a castle with the portcullis down, and those who gain entrance to that castle, in spite of the brave banners flying in the breeze and the lilies floating on the encircling moat which all look so gay, will be few.

Morris, in spite of his rich and abundant self-expression in all forms of art, was not an open or easy person. In a noble oak-tree we can see the increase of centuries: the height, the girth, the abundance of branches, the tapestry of leaves and acorns. We can see all these things, and admire and record—but we do not know the secret of that growth. The tree is dumb to us. In a sense, however wide spreading the branches of his works, Morris was also dumb.

Such achievements as those of Morris really belong to the heroic ages and not to the nineteenth century within the span of which he was born and died. They could only have been attained by a man built in an antique mould. Morris was such a man. All who knew him were agreed that he was greater than any of his works. "There's Morris," said Burne-Jones, "the larger half of that wonderful personality will perish when he dies." That has been proved true, yet much has survived. His outstanding personality speaks from his books (even though this modern generation may regard him as a purely "decorative" writer), and the pen was but one among his many tools

MORRIS: FROM THE PAINTING BY G. F. WATTS.

and weapons. In a sense he needs rescuing from his own exuberance. His name has a tendency to write itself in Black Letter, very heavy and Gothic, while twisted in and out of the letters is an elaborate scrollery of acanthus leaves and decorative flowers, as though pattern was a thing that existed in a dimension of its own, and could go on for ever, enchanted by its own evolutions. Amid this ordered and lavish pattern is seen not only the name but the person of William Morris—the very locks upon his head performing their own pattern-making.

But this outward exuberance was partly childlike and partly a kind of armour to his inner sensitiveness. In *News From Nowhere* he said: "It is the childlike part of us that produces works of imagination." Morris was one of the rare people who kept the child alive in him to "the ending of days", in that he never lost his eagerness and his joy in things, his desire to experiment with a new craft. It is the well-spring of the flowing freshness of his prose romances, which are so long and so truly "enchanted". He had the same delight in telling a tale that his master Chaucer had. The wish he expressed in his apostrophe to Chaucer which comes in his *Life and Death of Jason*, was surely granted:

> Would that I
> Had but some portion of that mastery
> That from the rose-hung lanes of woody Kent
> Through these five hundred years such songs have sent
> To us, who, meshed within this surly net
> Of unrejoicing labour, love them yet.
> And thou, O Master! Yea, my Master still,
> Whatever feet have scaled Parnassus' hill.

In telling his tales Morris had the same directness as Chaucer, the wish to tell them straight from the beginning to the end, without any of the breaks and elisions that the modern mind, in the modern terror of being bored, invents and uses. The great ancient stories of the world sufficed for Morris, because his nature was in tune with them and with all they sung and told. It seems that occasionally in the march of progress one will come who stays a little by the way and bids people pause and listen to the voice of the past. It is always poets or artists who call this halt, and often they are little heeded because of some lack of vitality in themselves which can bring no colour and no music out of that shadowy past. The practical man is inclined to scorn these often melancholy efforts—but no man, however practical, could scorn William Morris on that score, for his full-mouthed singing was but one among his abundant activities. He had almost as many crafts as there are methods of making things with hands. He was always of those that both do and know. He was naturally at home in the Middle Ages, which to him were times when men worked with their hands at many things and were inclined to sing whilst doing so. His attitude is shown in one of his sayings: "No one can draw armour properly unless he can draw a knight with his feet on the hob, toasting a herring on the point of his sword."

Beauty, to Morris, was not so much a thing you looked at and admired—except, of course, the beauty of nature— but a thing you *made*. There was no fun in it otherwise. He knew how the webs were woven, the yarns dyed, the stuffs embroidered, the beams carved and painted, the books set up and printed and bound. Knew, because he had done it all, and this vital difference of knowledge, the craftsman's, not the critic's knowledge, runs through all his descriptive writing. It must have been inborn in him —not from his immediate parents, but from some remoter ancestor—for as a grown man he easily and naturally became proficient in a craft which others had to learn toil-somely from their early youth. It was said at Morris's own works that unless a tapestry weaver starts as a lad he is never any real good at it. Yet Morris himself in his full maturity started not only to learn but to teach himself how to weave tapestry, and actually from his own experiments worked out the method of the old process, scorning to use the degraded modern technique. He had an upright loom erected in his bedroom at Kelmscott House—very typical of Morris, this, in his medieval disregard of what is called comfort—and used to rise earlier than most of the factory-workers of adjoining Hammersmith, and with his own wools wove on it a large tapestry of birds and acanthus leaves, which is a marvel of beauty and fine craftsmanship. It is common to apply the word genius to works of the imagination, and yet deny it to these inspirations of the hand and brain in unison. But genius is the only word that explains Morris's powers as a craftsman—not in one craft but in many.

When he wrote his early poems and stories Morris had not discovered—or at least not practised—this extraordinary gift. Therefore it is the more interesting to see how his early descriptive writing shadows it forth. The living minuteness of his accounts of how things were made is something more than literary. This was true of him all his life, in his later stories as in his early ones, as may be seen in his lovely description of how Birdalone in *The Water of the Wondrous Isles* embroidered her gown with flowers and branching tree-sprays, or how the master-mason of the *Unknown Church* built it and made it glorious with carven saints and angels. And there is an early essay of Morris's on the Cathedral of Amiens—how common a theme for the essay-writer are the cathedrals of England and France, and how dreary in most cases are these efforts!—but this passionate pæan of praise of the young William Morris is on another level. It is wonderful in its close and vivid imagery—it gives the full sense of the soaring Gothic splendours of the great edifice, and must be read breathless.

Much of medieval life was expressed in the glorious churches, and their beauty and the clamorous silver voices of their bells swinging in sunny belfries, pervade many of Morris's stories. In *The Hollow Land* there is a little vignette of the tolling of the great bell, Mary, which stays in the memory by reason of its simplicity and truth:

Far up in the dimness I saw the wheel before it began to swing round about; then it moved a little: the twelve men bent down to the earth, and a roar rose that shook the tower from base to spire-vane. Backwards and forwards swept the wheel, as Mary now looked downwards towards earth, now looked up on the shadowy cone of the spire, shot across by bars of light from the dormers.

This same *Hollow Land* is a wonderfully imagined little story, of the kind that is pure Morris, and was unique when it was created, though since then it has found many not always successful imitators, few of whom, however, can catch the simple-subtle note of the little song:

Christ keep the Hollow Land
All the summer-tide;
Still we cannot understand
Where the waters glide:

Only dimly seeing them
Coldly slipping through
Many green-lipped carven mouths,
Where the hills are blue.

Had Morris written nothing save his early stories and poems, and died as a young man when he had but lately gone down from Oxford, he yet would have been entitled to his place among English poets—though he himself made so little of it that when his poems were admired he said cheerfully: "Well, if this is poetry, it's very easy to write."

That saying is almost better than the poems—it shows his hearty sanity, his noble freedom from pose. It is true that these early poems belong to a world which is not this world, which never can have been this world, even in the thirteenth century—yet it is a world which is real and actual, because it is the world of Morris's real and acute imagination. It is Morris in his youth dreaming of a fair fantastic existence, and the dream is as deep as it is clear. But unlike most poets he was not content merely to dream of beauty. It is the essence of his greatness that he tried, through the whole of a full and hard-lived life, to make the dream come true. His poem, "The Message of the March Wind", could not have been written even by a great poet, unless he was in some sense a great man also. In it are mingled his passionate earth-feeling with the uprising in his soul of protest against the wrongs of his fellow men.

Morris's socialism, his preaching at street corners in the slums, was as much a part of his effort and striving to bring beauty, and with it happiness, to the world, as his poetry and his tapestry. We must admit it was the nobler part of his effort, inasmuch as the poetry and the tapestry were a joy to him, and the preaching at street corners was not. In an early letter he said, "My work is the embodiment of dreams in one form or another." But he was to find in his later years that the embodiment of dreams led him into the world, not into the clouds—and he was big enough to obey the call.

Bigness! That was at the root of all William Morris did and was. His enthusiasms, his capacity for work, his ideas and ideals, all were big. Burne-Jones expressed what he was to his friends—"A rock of defence to us all, and a castle on the top of it, and a banner on the top of that!" It is a splendid phrase, and a true one. Earlier Burne-Jones had said: "The like of him doesn't exist for dearness and goodness and simplicity—nothing like him ever was or will be." Burne-Jones probably knew Morris better than anybody in this world, and whatever he says about him is worthy of regard. Morris was, he says: "Strong, self-contained, master of himself, and therefore of the world. Solitude cannot hurt him nor dismay him."

Indeed, one of the convictions that increases through the study of Morris's life is that solitude is his natural setting. This in spite of the fact that so much of it was spent in company, in a young uproar of talk and plans and schemes for putting the world to rights; in later years

in constant contact with friends and with his own workmen and colleagues, with his wife and two daughters.
Through all this the inner love of solitude was intact,
though it was not till he discovered the Icelandic Sagas,
till he actually went to Iceland, that Morris really was
aware what he was made of, which was his own proper
country. It is a curious tale. The Man Who Found
Himself—so late. After his second visit to Iceland, in 1873,
Morris wrote: "The glorious simplicity of that terrible and
tragic but beautiful land, with its well-remembered stories
of brave men, killed all the querulous feeling in me . . . it
was no idle whim that drew me there, but a true instinct
for what I needed."

He had this true and deep instinct for what he needed
all his life. It guided him as a little boy in his wanderings
in Epping Forest, and in his first explorings in the thickets
of literature; it guided him in his ardent youth, and in his
not less ardent middle age; it guided him to the final
simplicities, when all the trappings and the banners were
left behind and he faced the stark Presence that, with a
medieval persistence, had to him always lurked behind
the roses and the arras, and crept among the Icelandic
rocks and mists. So vital, so rich in life, William Morris
never quite forgot, even in youth, that death comes in the
end. It was one reason why he always worked so hard
and unceasingly to accomplish all he might before the
night fell and the time came when he could work no more.
He who was always so eager to make and to see, who felt
the preciousness of time so acutely that it was a pain, never
found a way to "make quick-coming death a little thing".

Book One

YOUTH

I

In so many of the medieval romances and the older fairy-tales, a forest is the setting or the background to the lives and adventures of the hero. The castle, the court, the wood-cutter's cottage, are so often surrounded by untrodden depths of forest. This was only natural in a world where man had but hewn out his little clearings and townships from great stretches of land populated with trees—the uncharted greenwood was the natural margin to human existence in the early Middle Ages. So it is of a singular suitability that the story of William Morris begins with a forest—that of Epping.

When he was born in March 1834 Epping Forest had still a certain semblance to its medieval days, and therefore was the more suited to the needs and dreams of a most romantic small boy. The very names of his first two homes had a forest flavour—he was born at Elm House, Waltham-stow, and when he was six years old his parents moved to Woodford Hall, a large Georgian mansion set in fifty acres of park which ran into Epping Forest. Nothing save a wooden fence separated the Morris domain from the authentic forest—to a child there was no barrier between his home and the woods of faery. "Enter these enchanted woods, ye who dare."

The young William Morris, eldest son, though not eldest child, of a large family, naturally entered them on every possible occasion; the lure of the forest and the feel of it was part of his natural growth. "I was born and bred in its neighbourhood," he said in later years, "and when I was a boy and a young man knew it yard by yard from

Wanstead to the Theydons, and from Hale End to the Fairlop Oak. . . . The special character of it was derived from the fact that by far the greater part was a wood of hornbeams, a tree not common save in Essex and Herts. It was certainly the biggest hornbeam wood in these islands, and I suppose in the world. The said hornbeams were all pollards, being shrouded every four or six years, and were interspaced in many places with holly thickets. Nothing could be more interesting and romantic than the effect of the long poles of the hornbeams rising from the trunks and seen against the mass of the wood behind. It has a peculiar charm of its own not to be found in any other forest."

The ancestors of these hornbeams are believed to have been first imported from France after Agincourt, and planted in Epping Forest.

In later years memories of the Forest of Epping constantly reappear in Morris's poetry and prose tales. The forest had taken too deep a hold of his child imagination ever to depart from him. He had been born early enough to be a spectator and a hearer of some of the old Forest customs which had their roots in a remote past. He knew, as he said, the Fairlop Oak, which was later so ruthlessly destroyed and pulled up by attaching a great anchor to its roots—the Fairlop Oak which had so wide a spread of boughs that all the booths at the annual July Fair were covered by its green shade. The old Forest custom was still existent then, by which the commoners had the right of lopping for firewood from St. Martin's Day—this right being conditional on the lopping being begun as midnight struck on the day, and the first load of timber being then drawn away by a sledge pulled by white horses. Even if the small William Morris never saw this ceremony taking place, he would hear it talked about, and listen to the tales of old woodmen who had been there. Part of the Middle Ages was still in his actual world.

2

There is little in William Morris's immediate forebears
to account for his own special qualities and characteristics,
especially for his passionate love for beauty in all its shapes
and guises, whether in nature or in the works of men's
hands. Discussing this once with Wilfrid Scawen Blunt,
who was a friend of his later years, Morris said: "As for
me I have it naturally, for neither my father, nor my
mother, nor any of my relations had the least idea of it.
I remember as a boy going into Canterbury Cathedral and
thinking that the gates of heaven had been opened to me,
and also when I first saw an illuminated manuscript.
These first pleasures which I discovered for myself were
stronger than anything else I have had in my life."

Morris's parents, from the little that we know of them,
were excellent, honourable people, with the full panoply
of Victorian virtues; very comfortably off, securely enclosed
from all the disturbing aspects of life, whether too much
beauty, or too much misery. The Gorgon Head of Socialism
had not raised its grisly countenance in their placid world
—the Red Cap of Revolution which shook the generation
of Morris's grandparents had fortunately not crossed the
English Channel. In the comfortable Morris fortunes there
seemed but one little loophole of danger—a touch of the
Celt in some Welsh ancestry. Was it through that loophole
the "arrows of desire" penetrated to the heart of the small
William, making his life one continual quest for creative
work and visible beauty, for the crafts of the hand and the
dreams of the poet?

The fact that as a child he was delicate—in spite of the
robustness of his life in later years—set him just enough
apart from the daily round to give him his own special life,
which for the rest of his existence he clung to fiercely. At
the early age of seven years he had read all Scott's novels
to himself with enjoyment—rather an extraordinary

achievement. At eight, Gothic architecture became his first and abiding love. A light was lit in that child by his first sight of great building which never went out, and architecture to him from the first stood in her rightful place as the mother of the arts.

His childish years were happily set in the comfortable Georgian spaciousness of Woodford Hall, amid the hornbeams and the beeches of Epping Forest. The old and proper and natural ways of living were still in use there. The Morris family brewed their own beer, made their own butter, and baked their own bread. It was that bread Morris was remembering when he wrote in *News From Nowhere*, "The bread was particularly good . . . the big, rather close, dark-coloured, sweet-tasting farmhouse loaf."

The tastes and smells of childhood stay long in the memory—and also recollections of odd little things seen, like a picture of Abraham and Isaac worked in brown worsted, that hung on some wall at Woodford Hall, and a carved ivory Chinese ship with little gilded figures under a glass shade. In the library was a copy of the Tudor *Herbal* by John Gerarde, the rough enchanting woodcuts which illustrate the various plants made an impression on Morris which years later was reflected in his designs for chintzes and wallpapers.

Morris was remembering these rich early days when he wrote, in *News From Nowhere*: "When we are children time passes so slow with us that we seem to have time for everything." This may partly explain his immense output of work—for he kept all through his life that child quality. Always he was the child exploring the things in the world —so busy that he had not much time for human contacts, just like the absorbed child who turns a protective shoulder on an interfering presence.

Young William Morris had as many outdoor pursuits as indoor ones, and early acquired a taste for fishing, a sport which he continued to follow with unchanged satisfaction in his Kelmscott days, as many a memory of his friends later on recalls, with gleams of laughter woven among the memories—Morris was not a placid fisherman.

The kitchen-garden at Woodford Hall had natural attractions, and "the large blue plums which grow on the wall beyond the sweet-herb patch". All whose childish days were set in the country will share with him the memory of too-early bedtime. "To this day," he said, "when I smell a may-tree I think of going to bed by daylight."

It must always have been hard for him to go to bed when there were so many enchanting things waiting to be done. He had a pony to ride, the forest to explore, fish to catch, books to read—he used to read *The Old English Baron* in the rabbit warren at Woodford Hall with such intensity that he was scared to go home across the park.

At a very early age he developed a quite unusual and unchildish taste for old houses, churches, brasses. He may be said to have been born medieval, for it was certainly not cultivated in him by his comfortable home setting, except in so far as Woodford Hall was in reach of certain ancient Essex dwellings and churches. He was born also with a wonderful eye and memory. The things he had seen as a child he remembered without vagueness when he was a man. In a lecture he gave in 1882 on the "Lesser Arts of Life"—in which he said many things which must later be quoted, speaking with the full assurance of a proved craftsman—he gave a memory of his childhood. He was speaking of tapestry, that art which could "turn our chamber walls into the green woods of the leafy month of June, populous of bird and beast". He went on to say:

How well I remember as a boy my first acquaintance with a room hung with faded greenery at Queen Elizabeth's Lodge by Chingford Hatch, in Epping Forest (I wonder what has become of it now), and the impression of romance it made upon me; a feeling that always comes back on me when I read, as I often do, Sir Walter Scott's *Antiquary*, and come to the description of the Green Room at Monkbarns, amongst which the novelist has with such exquisite cunning of art imbedded the fresh and glittering verses of the summer poet Chaucer; yes, that was more than upholstery, believe me.

Architecture, the Mistress Art, spoke to him when still a child, and he never ceased to listen to her voice. Such was the young Morris, who enclosed in a material setting made comfortable by wealth and kindly ease, with an unusual amount of personal freedom seldom permitted to early Victorian children, made his own life very much on his own lines. This kind of stored life of his own always underlay his manifold and vigorous activities. Large numbers of his friends and fellow workers never even suspected it was there.

To a boy of this temperament and this inner strength, school life was not likely to mean a great deal—he had very little of the team spirit, or the games spirit. He always found the best game was making something, not chasing a ball.

It was fortunate for him that the public school to which he was sent was Marlborough, for Marlborough at that time was a very new public school and was in a somewhat chaotic state. There was little insistence on a rigid discipline and routine.

So young William Morris, the minimum of scholastic work accomplished—his good brain and good memory made such work easy to him—found himself at liberty to wander about the marvellous and ancient countryside surrounding Marlborough. His childhood had the background of Epping Forest; his adolescence that of Savernake Forest. He stepped backwards from the medieval to the prehistoric.

He was a great walker, and roamed about the country more or less as he liked, occasionally with a companion, more often by himself. And as he roamed he mused on the past of the country he walked over, and strove to unriddle the writings left on the Downs by early man, as well as studying the plainer script of village churches and farm and manor houses. Avebury made its mark on him, and Silbury Hill. In a letter of very scanty punctuation he wrote to his favourite elder sister Emma while he was still at Marlborough, given in full in Mackail's *Life*, Morris described a visit to Abury, as he called it, and Silbury in the spring of 1849:

On Monday I went to Silbury Hill, which I think I have told you before is an artificial hill made by the Britons but first I went to a place called Abury where there is a Druidical Circle and a Roman entrenchment both which encircle the town originally it is supposed the stones were in this shape first one large circle then a smaller one inside this and then one in the middle for an altar but a great many in fact most of the stones have been removed so I could not tell this. On Tuesday morning I was told of this so I thought I would go there again, I did and then I was able to understand how they had been fixed; I think the biggest stone I could see had about 16 feet out of the ground in height and about 10 feet thick and 12 feet broad the circle and entrenchment altogether is about half a mile; at Abury I also saw a very old church the tower was very pretty indeed it had four little spires on it of the decorated order, and there was a little Porch and inside the porch a beautiful Norman doorway loaded with mouldings.

It was all a part of his singular good fortune which sent Morris to school at Marlborough instead of to a harsher and older school—part of the fortune which gave him his kind and wealthy parents, his comfortable home on the edge of the ancient forest, his early delicacy, which later turned to vigorous health, his early freedom both from poverty and from constraint. Poverty has often enough been the nurse of genius; but Morris's nature needed no such spur to effort. He had money, and he used it freely, but he thought as little of it as of the rain that raineth every day. He never thought about it at all; there were so many more interesting things to think about.

While he was at Marlborough he was described by a schoolfellow as "a thick-set, strong-looking boy, with a high colour and black curly hair, good-natured and kind, but with a fearful temper."

The boys in his dormitory had the benefit of his gift for story-telling—night after night the endless Morris saga went on, a stream whose source never dried up. Thus early Morris began the story he was telling all his life. Also, while he was at school his hands showed their need to be always working at something. He began making nets, working incessantly at the job when he was not doing something else. His fingers hated being idle, were instinctively searching for the crafts in which later they were to excel. In that Marlborough schoolboy, with his constant netting and story-telling we see a fore-glimpse of the later Morris, seated at his tapestry loom or drawing-board, and making poetry in his head the while, saying that a fellow who couldn't do both together wasn't up to much.

3

While William Morris was still at Marlborough his father died, and his family decided to leave Woodford Hall and move to a slightly smaller but equally comfortable and commodious abode called Water House, Walthamstow. The name was bestowed upon it because of a broad moat at the back of the house which surrounded an island planted with aspen trees. The water was full of fish and the island full of romance. The fortunate Morris children fished and swam in the moat in summer and skated on it when the winter froze it. They learned to handle a boat; they camped and fished and cooked their catches on the island. It was an ideal setting for growing children—for their games and for their dreams, and William, who was fifteen at the time the move took place, absorbed it all deeply into his being.

It is a curious thing how his life was linked with water.

The names of his first two homes, Woodford Hall and Water House, indicate it; and his two last houses, Kelmscott House at Hammersmith, and Kelmscott Manor at Lechlade, were both beside the Thames. He was happy in a boat—he found his best relaxation in fishing, the smooth flow of a stream before his eyes. In an immature unpublished story Morris wrote jerkily and clumsily, yet with obvious truth, of a boy who was plainly a memory of himself:

> You know one has fits of not caring for fishing and shooting a bit, and then you get through an enormous lot of reading; and then again one day one goes out and down to the river and looks at the eddies, and then suddenly one thinks of all that again; and then another day when one has one's rod in one's hand one looks up and down the field or sees the road winding along, and I can't help thinking of the tales going on amongst it all, and long so for more and more books.

That "one"—"all alone"—with his rod in his hand, his uncertainties, his dreams, his longing for all the tales in the world, is just the boy William Morris beginning his quest for the "well at the world's end", and the "wood beyond the world"—trees and water, the forest and the river. The troubadour within him was stirring; the melancholy of early youth was adding strange cloud colours to his familiar happy landscape. The robust and the delicate are curiously mingled in William Morris: the delicate inevitably retreating behind the robust as he grew older; it is only youth that has no armour. His almost complete silence about his inmost personal feelings, those feelings which lay beneath the flowing freedom of his utterances in prose and poetry, was Morris's way of protecting himself. It was as though in order to express himself at all he had to go backwards into another age, to dress up in Grecian or medieval clothes, so that none might guess at him too closely. It was only in his latter years, when he had found the strange stark country where he was at home,

where there were no battlemented towers, no curtain walls
and keeps, no moats or portcullized gateways, only the
black rocks and craters of Iceland, with ancestral voices
calling on the wind, that he shed his protective poetical
trappings and wrote his greatest poem, *Sigurd the
Volsung*.

4

When Morris left Marlborough he went to Oxford, and
not unnaturally for a Marlborough boy, to the West
Country College of Exeter. But as his natural tastes were
not classical, and the distinctly undisciplined freedom of
Marlborough while he was there had not kept his nose
unduly to the grindstone, before he went up to Oxford
some of the gaps were filled by a year's tutoring with the
Reverend F. B. Grey, later Canon of St. Albans. His
tutor, of a scholarly and attractive disposition, with whom
Morris continued a friendship in adult years, was what
was then known as a High Churchman. It was partly his
influence, combined with that of his favourite sister Emma,
who about this time married a young High Church curate,
that made the youthful William Morris consider the
Church as his probable future career. That was his idea
when he went up to Oxford, and at Exeter he met for the
first time another young man who also intended to enter
the Church, whose name was Edward Burne-Jones.

If contrast is a cause of attraction these two were destined
for friendship. Morris, very broad and powerful, had
quite outgrown his early delicacy. He was inclined to be
thick-set, and never grew very tall. He was ruddy of
countenance and violent in his movements. He was fond
of fencing, but made such wild rushes that it was necessary
to put some obstacle, such as a small table, between him
and his opponent. He broke things almost unconsciously.
Few chairs survived his usage; he had a way of tilting them

backwards and twisting his legs among the rungs that no joiner's work could stand up to. His hair waved and curled on his head like a banner—a sign of his exuberant vitality —and very early in life he ceased to shave and added an exuberant beard to his exuberant mop.

There is an early and rather bad drawing of Morris by himself (reproduced in the first volume of his *Collected Works*, edited by his daughter May Morris) without a date, but showing him with his wild hair subdued, a small moustache half hiding his sensitive mouth; his eyes looking very Tennysonian and melancholy. It might easily have been a portrait of any cultivated and poetic-minded young man of the period, except for a hint of the peculiar Morris quality in the eyes. But superficially this may have been the face into which Burne-Jones looked—though the fire is missing—on that long-past day at Oxford when these two first met. A meeting that was to mean so much to them both for the rest of their lives.

What Morris would see was the physical opposite of himself: a young man thinner and taller than he was, a little drooping in the carriage of the head and shoulders; pale, fair-haired, quiet, rather shy. There is much that is characteristic of Edward Burne-Jones in a joke he made in one of his letters to William De Morgan in later years complaining that they had not met for so long:

> I wish I could see you, time is slipping by horribly. I suppose we shall meet as Bogies—and if you promise not to frighten me I will promise not to frighten you! No hiding behind doors, mind, I can't stand it, my nerves, never of the best, are not likely to be better then!

He was very fond of drawing what he called "bogy pictures"—some of them distinctly creepy—and there was a faint bogy touch about him, the look of one not quite at home in this world, shrinking and faintly apprehensive.

Max Beerbohm, with his inimitable eye for character, has put the Morris–Burne-Jones qualities on record for posterity in the picture he calls "Topsy and Ned Jones Seated on the Settle in Red Lion Square". Of course this depicts a later period in their friendship than the early days at Oxford, but its essential truth, as well as its wit, is timeless and permanent. Morris and Burne-Jones are shown seated on a massive hand-hewn settle—Morris had by then recognized the necessity of acquiring a type of Stone Age furniture which would not collapse under his habitual usage. The solid settle is decorated with Burne-Jones's paintings of wan angels and medieval damsels. On a substantial kitchen table beside the settle is a bottle of Bass's beer and a cottage loaf—perhaps it is a Max Beerbohm British version of the famous Persian verse, the "thou" being represented by the lanky Burne-Jones, who is nervously squeezed into one corner of the settle, clutching at his limp, pale beard, while he listens apprehensively to the poem Morris is reading fiercely aloud. Morris's broad figure occupies nearly the whole of the settle, and his black locks stand up with furious vigour, like the snakes of Medusa. Burne-Jones's air of nervousness is fully justified.

The cartoon is as funny as it is witty, for it really sums up the relations and characteristics of the two men, who for all the remaining years of their lives were so deeply devoted to each other. Morris always took up a good deal of room, and Burne-Jones shoved himself into corners. Morris was large, pugnacious, a born fighter; Burne-Jones was precisely the opposite. Morris was naturally a leader; Burne-Jones as naturally a recluse. The strong link between them was that they were both artists, both "dreamers of dreams"; Burne-Jones looked the part, Morris did not, but under the superficial differences each knew what the other was made of, and they never failed or misunderstood each other, from the time of their first meeting in 1853 to the time of Morris's death in 1896. Not even the fact that the young Morris had wealth and the young Burne-Jones had not, made any difference to them. Few men have ever lived who thought less of money than Morris—it was not

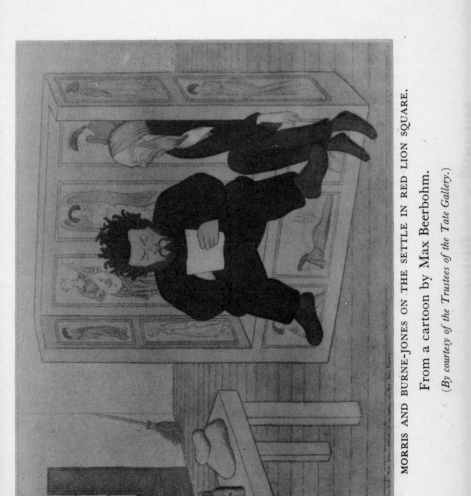

MORRIS AND BURNE-JONES ON THE SETTLE IN RED LION SQUARE.

From a cartoon by Max Beerbohm.

one of the things he ever considered worthy of thought.
He had never known the inconvenience of not possessing
it, but the only gold that ever glittered for him was that
shining in the flowers and haloes of an illuminated medieval
missal or book of hours; for that kind of gold he would give
many commercial sovereigns. That gold in itself had any
importance, that a man could pride himself on the mere
fact of possessing it, was not an idea that ever dawned on
his mind. Indeed, it was only in his later years that he
realized how the *lack* of it embittered the lives of so many
—and then, characteristically, he took action about it, to
the great disturbance of most of his friends. That was the
only matter in which he and Burne-Jones did not see
as brothers.

5

But all these questions were in the far future when
Morris and Burne-Jones began their lives at Oxford
together. No setting could have been more suitable for
their friendship. At that date Oxford was on the verge
of great and tragic changes in the way of building and
modernization, but those changes had hardly begun, in
spite of the coming of the railway. Burne-Jones could say:

> On all sides except where it touched the railway the City
> came to an end abruptly as if a wall had been about it, and
> you came suddenly upon the meadows. There was little brick
> in the City; it was either grey with stone, or yellow with the
> wash of the pebble-cast in the poorer streets, where there were
> still many old houses with wood carving, and a little sculpture
> here and there.

He said that to him and Morris the buildings of Merton
and the cloisters of New College were their "chief shrines
in Oxford".

To Morris the University was "a vision of grey-roofed

houses and a long winding street, and the sound of many bells". He had a medieval love for bells, and though his Gothic soul early developed a dislike for the work of Sir Christopher Wren and his followers, the bell that rings 101 strokes in Wren's Tom Tower every night at nine o'clock came from Osney Abbey, and it is not difficult to imagine the young Morris standing on a moonlit night in the famous Tom Quad, on one side of him the magnificent Christ Church Hall, whose "line of festal light" the Scholar-Gipsy "turn'd once to watch", counting the hundred and one strokes with joy.

Years afterwards Morris said of the time when he was at Oxford:

> Oxford in those days still kept a great deal of its earlier loveliness; and the memory of its grey streets as they then were has been an abiding influence and pleasure in my life, and would be greater still if I could only forget what they are now —a matter of far more importance than the so-called learning of the place could have been to me in any case, but which, as it was, no one tried to teach me, and I did not try to learn.

The lovely country round about, the river, and the enchanting villages, he explored and studied with his acutely observing eye, and stored away in his capacious memory. And young as he was, William Morris knew what he wanted from life—and also, with equal determination, what he did not want. Burne-Jones said of him:

> Just as in after years, in the thick of his work, it was noticeable how he never seemed to be particularly busy, and how he had plenty of leisure for expeditions, for fishing, for amusement, if it amused him; he never seemed to read much, but always knew, and accurately; and he had a great instinct at all times for knowing what would not amuse him, and what not to read.

To an undergraduate of this temper Exeter offered almost the same attractive laxness of discipline as Marlborough had offered the schoolboy. It was overcrowded:

the Rector was non-resident and ill. How little Morris's own tutor appreciated his qualities is shown by his statement that Morris was "a rather rough and unpolished youth, who exhibited no special literary tastes and capacity, but had no difficulty in mastering the usual subjects of examination". As though one who had only handled a chestnut burr declared there could be nothing smooth and shining within.

The effect on Morris of this careless indifference was not good. For the rest of his life he was scornful on the subject of University education, and the name of don was used by him, says Mackail, "as a synonym for all that was narrow, ignorant, and pedantic".

"Little by little", said Burne-Jones of himself and Morris, "we fed ourselves with the food that fitted us."

The real reason Morris and Burne-Jones had come to Oxford, had they but known it, was not for purposes of acquiring a scholastic education, but to meet and educate each other. Burne-Jones describes him at this time:

> He talked with vehemence, and sometimes with violence. I never knew him languid or tired. He was slight in figure in those days; his hair was dark brown and very thick, his nose straight, his eyes hazel-coloured, his mouth exceedingly delicate and beautiful.

These two, though friendly with a certain number of other men, especially a Birmingham set connected with Burne-Jones, withdrew into an inner citadel of their own. Their kindred interests, their kindred careers—both intending to enter the Church—locked and bolted the door on outsiders. Behind that spiritually sported oak they read and they talked continuously. Morris, wrote Burne-Jones on one occasion, "came tumbling in and talked incessantly for the next seven hours or longer". He was quite capable of it when in the mood. And if not talking he liked reading aloud, though he could not bear anyone reading aloud to him. But Burne-Jones delighted in Morris's reading. In

2

this way they read together Milman's *Latin Christianity*,
large portions of the *Acta Sanctorum*, and the *Tracts for the
Times*, Neale's *History of the Eastern Church*, as well as Sis-
mondi, and medieval chronicles and Latin poetry. The
influence of all this ecclesiastical and medieval study nearly
took Morris into what seemed the natural home of this
medieval young man, the Roman Catholic Church.

But gradually the ecclesiastical reading became per-
meated by other interests—by poetry, by mythology, by
art, and by the powerful influence of Ruskin's *Modern
Painters*. Ruskin and Tennyson were great prophets in those
days. Ruskin was destined to influence Burne-Jones's life
more strongly than that of Morris, but *Modern Painters* was
important to them both, and the chapter from *The Stones of
Venice* on the "Nature of Gothic" always held his admiration, and in time to come was reprinted by him at the
Kelmscott Press. In the preface he wrote for it he said:

> To my mind, and I believe to some others, it is one of the
> most important things written by the author, and in future
> days will be considered as one of the very few necessary and
> inevitable utterances of the century. . . . For the lesson which
> Ruskin here teaches us, is that art is the expression of man's
> pleasure in labour; that it is possible for man to rejoice in his
> work, for, strange as it may seem to us to-day, there have been
> times when he did rejoice in it; and lastly, that unless man's
> work once again becomes a pleasure to him the token of which
> change will be that beauty is once again a natural and necessary
> accompaniment of productive labour, all but the worthless
> must toil in pain, and therefore live in pain. So that the result
> of the thousands of years of man's effort on the earth must be
> general unhappiness and universal degradation—unhappiness
> and degradation, the conscious burden of which will grow in
> proportion to the growth of man's intelligence, knowledge, and
> power over material nature.

This was written within four years of Morris's death, so
his young view of its value had not changed. But he was
to show very soon that he himself could write as finely on

"the nature of Gothic" as anyone then living, indeed with
a craftsman's grasp of the actual technique of building that
Ruskin could never claim.

That was one of the extraordinary things about Morris
which his friends began about this time to notice with
astonishment; he knew how things were done, even before
he began to make many of them himself. Burne-Jones said
he did not read it up, he just knew instinctively. It seemed
as though the craftsmen of half a dozen or more medieval
"trades" were reincarnated in him.

Not only Ruskin, but also Carlyle, on the strength of his
Past and Present, was regarded as a prophet by these young
men, though it is very odd to think that at this early time
Morris was not acquainted with those two medieval writers
he was a little later to worship so ardently—Chaucer and
Malory. But it is equally odd to remember that at this
time another book which he did know and love was
Charlotte Yonge's *Heir of Redclyffe*—that pious, melancholy,
Victorian novel seems on the face of it little likely to appeal
to the medieval-minded Morris. But one of the things
which is peculiarly appealing about him during the whole
of his life is that he was never sophisticated, never "clever",
never afraid to like what he liked lest he be despised by
"superior persons". Not that he was the only one in his
set to admire the *Heir of Redclyffe*—they all of them did—
and one of them, Dixon, pronounced it long after his
Oxford days as "unquestionably one of the finest books in
the world".

In Mackail's admirable *Life of William Morris* there are
several pages written by Dixon, who was a Pembroke man,
about the set which was gradually forming the nucleus of
the Brotherhood—Dixon himself, Cornell Price, William
Fulford, Charles Faulkner, and of course, Burne-Jones and
Morris. "At first," Dixon says,

> Morris was regarded by the Pembroke men simply as a very
> pleasant boy (the least of us was senior by a term to him)

who was fond of talking, which he did in a husky shout, and fond of going down the river with Faulkner, who was a good boating man. He was very fond of sailing a boat. In no long time, however, the great character of his nature began to impress us. His fire and impetuosity, great bodily strength, and high temper were soon manifested: and were sometimes astonishing. . . . But his mental qualities, his intellect, also began to be perceived and acknowledged. I remember Faulkner remarking to me, "How Morris seems to know things, doesn't he?" And then it struck me that it was so. I observed how decisive he was: how accurate, without any effort or formality: what an extraordinary power of observation lay at the back of many of his casual or incidental remarks, and how many things he knew that were quite out of our way; as, e.g., architecture. One of the first things he ever said to me was to ask me to go with him to look at Merton Tower.

A little later in the course of these reminiscences of youth, Canon Dixon said:

At this time Morris was an aristocrat, and a High Church-man. His manners and tastes and sympathies were all aristo-cratic. His countenance was beautiful in feature and expression, particularly in the expression of purity. Occasionally it had a melancholy look. He had a finely cut mouth, the short upper lip adding greatly to the purity of expression. I have a vivid recollection of the splendid beauty of his presence at this time.

6

Morris's tastes and ideals in this heyday of his youth were as splendid as his presence. Poetry, architecture, romantic history, were his pursuit and passion. He was not alone in this; the University at that time was swept by a passion for poetry, particularly the poetry of Tennyson, which to most of the poetry-reading undergraduates seemed the final achievement and crown of the English muse. But

Morris, so soon to burgeon as a poet himself, had a certain half humorous, half critical reserve as to this; he had a "defiant admiration"—he did not think that all which Tennyson wrote was quite perfect. He felt that Tennyson's Sir Galahad was too mild a youth, and the hero of "Locksley Hall" a bit rowdy. Nevertheless, he shared the general admiration, and all these ardent young men recited poetry and talked poetry by day and by night.

Morris, as has been said, liked reading aloud. There are different opinions extant as to his reading of poetry. When it was his own poetry it seems generally agreed that he read it gruffly—rather in the manner of throwing a bone at a dog, as though saying, "Take it, or leave it, I don't care!"—without any graces of delivery. This may be explained by the shyness of the young poet, awkward at any display of the heart on his sleeve.

This, of course, would not apply to the poetry of other men, or only in a much less degree. Shakespeare readings were started in each other's rooms, and according to Dixon both Morris and Burne-Jones were fine readers. "I remember", he said,

> Morris's Macbeth, and his Touchstone particularly; but most of all his Claudio, in the scene with Isabel. He suddenly raised his voice to a loud and horrified cry at the word "Isabel", and declaimed the awful following speech, "Aye, but to die, and go we know not where", in the same pitch. I never heard anything more overpowering.

Then Morris suddenly began to write poetry himself. All his friends were surprised. He apparently just sat down and did it, as naturally as he might have sat down and eaten his dinner. His most intimate friend, Burne-Jones, was just as surprised as everybody else.

One morning after breakfast Topsy—or Top, as by this time he had been christened owing to his massive mop of hair, and continued to be called by his intimates for the rest of his life—brought from his rooms in the Old Buildings

of Exeter to Burne-Jones in the same Buildings the first
poem he had written. It was called "The Willow and the
Red Cliff". Burne-Jones was astounded. When some other
men came in he called out to them wildly:

"He's a big poet!"

"Who is?" they asked.

"Why, Topsy."

They heard him read the poem aloud, and one of the
hearers wrote afterwards:

> It was a thing entirely new: founded on nothing previous:
> perfectly original, whatever its value, and something truly
> striking and beautiful, extremely decisive and powerful in
> execution. It must be remembered particularly that it was
> the first piece of verse that he had ever written; there was no
> novitiate; and not a trace of influence; and then it will
> be acknowledged that this was an unprecedented thing. He
> reached his perfection at once.

It was amid all this chorus of praise that Morris made his
classically casual remark: "Well, if this is poetry, it's very
easy to write."

Nobody now can read that poem, for it is destroyed and
vanished. But we can read another early poem of his,
which also would have been lost had a copy of it not been
preserved in a letter Morris wrote to "Crom" Price,
enclosing the poem, though declaring it was "exceedingly
seedy":

'Twas in church on Palm Sunday,
Listening what the priest did say
Of the kiss that did betray,

That the thought did come to me
How the olives used to be
Growing in Gethsemane:

That the thoughts upon me came
Of the lantern's steady flame,
Of the softly whispered name;

Of how kiss and words did sound
When the olives stood around,
While the robe lay on the ground.

Then the words the Lord did speak,
And that kiss in Holy Week
Dreams of many a kiss did make:

. . . .

Kiss upon the death-bed given,
Kiss on dying forehead given
When the soul goes up to Heaven.

Many thoughts beneath the sun
Thought together: Life is done,
Yet for ever life doth run.

Willow standing 'gainst the blue
Where the light clouds come and go
Mindeth me of kiss untrue.

Christ thine awful cross is thrown
Round the whole world, and thy Sun
Woeful kisses looks upon.

Eastward slope the shadows now,
Very light the wind does blow,
Scarce it lifts the laurels low;

I cannot say the things I would,
I cannot think the things I would,
How the Cross at evening stood.

Very blue the sky above,
Very sweet the faint clouds move,
Yet I cannot think of love.

That little poem, touched with a curious medieval grace
and simplicity, tells us a good deal about the young Morris,
and shows how, at twenty-two, he was already the man he

was to become. His qualities were all there, a little callow and gasping as they emerge from the shell.

There is a photograph taken when he was twenty-three, which also tells us something about him. Throughout his life he was photographed a number of times, and though photography of the period from 1858 to 1890 was on the whole very pedestrian and lacking in charm, it had a plain satisfactory quality as a record which perhaps is of more value than the highly temperamental studies of modern photographic artists, where the sitter lurks in shadows so deep or so distorted that little emerges save a gleaming eye or the jut of a chin. In this photograph of Morris when he was twenty-three years of age, he sits solemnly at a photographer's table, his right hand on a book, in a suit as respectable as an undertaker's, save for the vast black bow-tie which nearly hides his collar. His curly hair is brushed as far as possible into order, he has a tiny moustache and a slight fringe of whisker round his chin. His expression is an odd mixture of dreaminess and anger, rather as though he had been taken from some loved pursuit and made to sit before the camera, and was in consequence inwardly seething. In spite of his youth it is not a young face, in spite of a certain unworldly look. The eyes, as always, stand out because of their peculiar, characteristic expression.

7

To his friends at this time young William Morris must have seemed a singularly fortunate person. He was obviously gifted, attractive, full of virile health and vigour—indeed, in vigour he was abounding—he was in an unusual degree free to direct his own life, and he had plenty of money. When he was twenty-one he came into £900 a year of his own—in those days a very considerable income. But much more important than these fair worldly circumstances was what lay underneath in Morris's mind. A sentence in a letter to "Crom" Price tells us a great deal more about him than any statement of his income: "I mean", he wrote to his friend, "that most beautiful poetry, and indeed almost all beautiful writing makes one feel sad or indignant."

Why "indignant", it may be asked? But it is just that word which marks out Morris from the rest of his friends and associates. They were, like him, responsive to beauty in most of its manifestations, and conscious of the sadness, the "sense of tears", that lurks behind all beauty. But Morris was indignant as well. That word—probably at the time he did not exactly know why he used it, or did not understand the feeling that made him use it—was to grow as he grew. It was a seed which was to bear unexpected fruit in future years.

Morris's first journey abroad to France and Belgium was a notable part of his education. It took place in his second Long Vacation, that of 1854. He who as a child of eight had been smitten to the soul by Canterbury Cathedral, missed nothing of the magnificence of the French churches he saw: of Amiens, Beauvais, and Chartres. He saw, too, for the first time, the paintings of Van Eyck and Memling. The whole journey was a revelation to him of things he had only dreamed about, never before beheld with his bodily eyes. As his knowledge and his taste increased and settled with the years, his most passionate loves among all the works of men's hands were the greatest and the least— Gothic architecture and illuminated manuscripts. His early love for architecture began when he was no more than a child; a minor manifestation of this was his school-boy passion for going "a-brassing", as he called taking rubbings of church brasses. When he was still a very young man he wrote an account of Amiens Cathedral, which is a pæan of joy, and a strange little architectural tale called "The Story of the Unknown Church". "I think", he wrote, "these same churches of North France the grandest, the

most beautiful, the kindest and most loving of all the earth
has ever borne."

He wrote with full and rejoicing detail of the great
cathedral of Amiens:

> I felt inclined to shout when I first entered Amiens Cathedral.
> It is so fine and vast and noble that I did not feel in the least
> awestruck or humbled·by its size and grandeur; I have not
> often felt thus when looking on architecture, but have felt, at
> all events at first, intense exultation at the beauty of it. That,
> and a certain kind of satisfaction in looking on the geometrical
> tracery of the windows, on the sweep of the large arches, were,
> I think, my first feelings in Amiens Cathedral.

An important event in the following year of 1855 was
that Morris and Burne-Jones read through the whole of
Chaucer together. There was a deep kinship between
Chaucer and Morris, which is shown as his life developed,
and was crowned most fittingly by the last work of his life,
the great Kelmscott Press *Chaucer*. That book, just completed, was given into his hands only a short time before
his death; it would have been an ill hap had he not lived
long enough to see and handle it, to look with loving eyes
at the borders and initial letters, at the type he had designed for it—was Caxton looking over his shoulder?—at
the illustrations done by his early Oxford friend Burne-
Jones. Everything was linked up and finished perfectly:
the circle that began in 1854 was completed in 1896, and
at the end, as at the beginning, a river flowed by—the Isis
at Oxford where the young men sat reading the enchanting
prologue to the *Canterbury Tales*, the Thames at Hammersmith, where the dying Morris sat looking at his last book,
his last work, his *Chaucer*.

8

The not unnatural result of this widening and deepening of outside interests, this up-growing of the art and poetry of their inner natures, was that both Burne-Jones and Morris were beginning to feel that the Church was no longer their destined vocation. It is a little amusing to consider how completely unorthodox a parson Morris would have made, how all his parishioners would have been set spinning and block-printing, and how Burne-Jones would have drooped under the recital of the woes of the village mothers—the children's coughs and burns, the injuries they had received from their neighbours' tongues.

But they were preserved from the fate of their gifts being stultified, and one of the most potent influences in preventing this was Dante Gabriel Rossetti.

It is impossible to ignore Rossetti in writing of either Morris or Burne-Jones, in spite of a certain wish to do so, for Rossetti has had an undue share of attention in the consideration of those interested in the Pre-Raphaelites. His works, his self-pity, his poems dedicated to a grave and then dug up again, his "temperament", his extravagance, his drug-taking, his selfishness, have cast a certain shadow over the younger and greater man, William Morris. Even if unconsciously, there was much of the vampire in Rossetti —he lived on the vitality of those who admired him, and such a relationship can never be good. Morris, as he grew older, began to see this very clearly, and at last burst the bonds which fettered his own strength. He may not have gone quite as far as Samuel Butler, who said of Rossetti, "I dislike his face, and his manner, and his work, and I hate his poetry, and his friends". But the severance, when it came, was final.

Burne-Jones, as being more malleable and gentler than Morris, partly also because he was first and last a painter, not a man of many trades like "Topsy", remained longer under Rossetti's spell.

But in the beginning Rossetti's influence was a marvel to those not very mature young men, and they flocked about him and regarded everything he taught as gospel. There was work and fun, and the dawning of a new world. With Rossetti there was the first attempt at decorative art in the medieval manner in the communal painting of the Oxford Union, where the frescoes, owing to lack of technical knowledge, so soon faded. There was probably the only occasion on which Morris, who was born a craftsman, did an ineffective job of work. His rule was to find out for himself how to do a thing before he did it; and the remarkable thing about him was that in the handling of so many different crafts he seemed to have an instinctive knowledge as to how the things were made and done.

His equipment for life was unusual in that he had both the head and the hands—two gifts that commonly do not go together. The output and quality of his poetry would alone constitute a sufficient career: and yet poetry, compared with his other pursuits, was hardly more than the mortar with which he filled in the interstices between the solid blocks of stone with which he built his house of life. And he was a master-man at all his jobs, doing and making with his own hands.

By the end of his Oxford career Morris finally decided that the Church was not for him. In a letter to his mother telling her of his decision, he said: "You see I do not hope to be great at all in anything, but perhaps I may reasonably hope to be happy in my work, and sometimes when I am idle and doing nothing, pleasant visions go past me of the things that may be."

The career he had chosen, as being concerned with things for which he cared passionately, was architecture. In January 1856 he was articled to G. E. Street, and went into his Oxford office. To his work as an articled clerk there he decided, on Rossetti's insistent urging, that he would add painting in his spare time.

Burne-Jones had decided to be a painter pure and simple. By this choice Burne-Jones was settled for life, but not so Morris—he was not a painter in Rossetti's meaning of the word. He was a decorative designer, he was an illuminator of books, but he was not a painter of pictures in oils and water-colours. If he wanted to paint a picture he would do it in words, or in embroidery silks:

> Lo, silken my garden
> And silken my sky,
> And silken my apple boughs
> Hanging on high;
>
> All wrought by the worm
> In the peasant Carle's cot
> On the mulberry leafage
> When summer was hot.

For a time, however, he thought he was on the right road—always more difficult to find for a young man who has no urgent monetary reason to work for his living.

It was in Street's office at Oxford that he met Philip Webb, the chief clerk there, who was to become his lifelong friend. One of Morris's marked good fortunes was his habit of meeting the people he needed at the right time; he did not, owing to his natural self-completeness, need many people, but it seems that those he needed he unfailingly met. Burne-Jones was essentially and supremely one of those people; Philip Webb was another. And so was Jane Burden, in her degree.

In the same month and year in which Morris began his professional study of architecture the first number of the *Oxford and Cambridge Magazine* appeared. It ran for twelve monthly numbers, and then, as is the way of such publications, deceased.

This magazine professed to be the work of hands from

both Universities, but actually it was an Oxford product, and largely owed its existence to Morris. He wrote in every one of the twelve monthly numbers, sometimes two stories and a poem in one number, save for the two months of June and July; and almost the entire cost of production was paid out of his generous pocket. The young architect beginning his toil in Street's office was also the monetary magnate financing that expensive hobby—a private magazine. We can only admire this extremely industrious young man, studying architecture with his right hand and painting with his left, and in between whiles taking to his pen as easily as the young duck takes to water.

It was at the end of this important year that Morris wrote the well-known words in which he declared that he had no political interests, though "I see that things are in a muddle, and I have no power or vocation to set them right in ever so little a degree. My work is the embodiment of dreams in one form or another."

In that very denial stirs something deep within him which, later on, was to bear surprising fruit.

9

Morris's contributions to the *Oxford and Cambridge Magazine* during the year of its existence—apart from his financial support, in which he "hoped not to lose more than £300"— were numerous, and range from slight descriptive sketches like the account of Retzel's "Death the Avenger" and "Death the Friend", eulogy of Browning's poetry, description of the "Churches of North France", and the "Story of the Unknown Church", already referred to, and an absurd Victorian tale, "Frank's Sealed Letter", which yet contains, very incongruously, the following haunting little poem.

Wearily, drearily,
Half the day long,
Flap the great banners
High over the stone;
Strangely and eerily
Sounds the wind's song
Bending the banner poles.

While all alone
Watching the loophole's spark
Lie I with life, all dark,
Fast tethered, hands fettered
Fast to the stone,
The grim walls square-lettered
With prisoned men's groan.
Still strain the banner-poles
Through the wind's song,
Westward the banner rolls
Over my wrong.

That is pure Morris, a foretaste of what he was to be. But some of his contributions to the *Oxford and Cambridge Magazine* are engagingly young, like the shy and stiffly expressed article on Browning, with its generous indignation about the poet's detractors; poetry being, as Morris says, "one of the very grandest of all God's gifts to men". In the final paragraph of this essay he writes rather like a schoolboy:

Yes, I wonder what the critics would have said to *Hamlet, Prince of Denmark* if it had been first published by Messrs. Chapman & Hall in the year 1855.

Very youthful, too, is the artless ending of "Golden Wings" when the knight describes his own death: "and as I fell forward one cleft me to the teeth with his axe."

Nevertheless it was true, as Burne-Jones said in 1855:

Watch carefully all that Morris writes. You will find one of the very purest and most beautiful minds on earth breathing through all he touches.

It was in this University magazine that Morris in those early days began to write the first of those half medieval, half fairy-tale romances, which in later years became one of the most individual fruits of his genius. These early stories are: "A Dream", "Gertha's Lovers", "Svend and His Brethren", "Lindenborg Pool", "The Hollow Land", and "Golden Wings".

These romances show several things about Morris—what an acute and sensitive eye he had, joined to a faithful memory of things seen and heard; what a natural skill with words, and, in spite of certain archaisms inevitable in one of his temperament, he had also the grace of a simple Saxon diction. But though he early showed that he could construct a tale, decorate it lavishly, give it atmosphere and a certain remote loveliness, the knights and their ladies, the wise old men, the wicked queens, are but painted figures, not human beings. So it was in later days when he was designing tapestries; the gorgeous and intricate backgrounds are his, the figures were all limned by Burne-Jones or some other hand. It was all really part of his temperament; human beings (with few exceptions) came quite a long way down in the list of his interests.

That early experiment in the writing of pure disembodied romance lasted for only about a year, and from then onwards for nearly thirty years everything he wrote was poetry.

This was largely due to the tremendous influence of Chaucer upon him—Chaucer, whom he hailed as his master and in whose golden steps he naturally wished to travel. There he found "God's plenty", and he took what belonged to him. But Chaucer's humour and delight in common men and common life was never his, in spite of his socialistic ideas and aims in later years. Morris, in his youth, had an uproarious sense of fun, but it was quite different from Chaucer's sly and mellow brand of humour. Actually it was much more Malory than Chaucer who was stamped on these first romances of Morris. It is very

odd to recall that not till he was twenty-two years old did
he and his friend Burne-Jones first come upon the *Morte
d'Arthur.*

Burne-Jones found the volume first at Cornish's book-
shop in Birmingham, a leisurely, old-fashioned establish-
ment, where the customers could wander about and browse
happily among the crowded shelves, a great boon to the
impoverished book-lover. Burne-Jones found Malory's
history there; he could not afford to buy it, but spent hours
reading in it at intervals, occasionally, as he said, pacifying
the bookseller and justifying his constant presence by buying a cheaper volume. Then one day "Topsy" came along,
was introduced to the incomparable treasure, and at once
bought it, so that he and Ned Burne-Jones could enchant
themselves with it together at all hours of the night and
day. It became one of their fundamental books.

Morris's years at Oxford gave him a great deal in
giving him Chaucer and Malory, who were to remain
major influences in his life. Oxford also gave him his
principal friends and his wife. A man could hardly ask
for more.

He and Burne-Jones had many ideal dreams of friendship, of founding a Brotherhood. In the first idea it was
to be a religious community, at the time when they were
both contemplating going into the Church, and used regu-
larly with other kindred spirits to practise singing and
plain-chant in Holywell. Then it was to be a brotherhood of artists, and for long enough they used the name
to express the link between them, till marriage and the
necessities of supporting their families ended it. But the
spirit of brotherhood continued unchanged in some few
of their hearts, notably those of "Topsy" and Ned Burne-
Jones. With them it was always there, under whatever
other pursuits and interests and friendships they might be
involved. This knowledge of a deep comradeship must
have been in Morris's mind when he made John Ball
say the following.

Forsooth he that waketh in hell and feeleth his heart fail him shall have memory of the merry days of youth, and how that when his heart faileth him there he cried on his fellow, and how that his fellow heard him and came.

So would those two have gone to hell at the call of need from the other.

10

After Morris took his Bachelor's Degree at Oxford he ceased to shave, and began to show the world thus early in his life the familiar aspect of bearded face and unruly mop of curly hair that all but the earliest portraits display. He would certainly have had less of the time he valued so greatly if he had adopted the practice of shaving his face —it was quite enough to keep the riotous growth of hair and beard within the bounds permitted to an artist. In one of his early poems Morris wrote of a knight who was shut long in castle prison, till as he looked out of his narrow window:

> There was not room for all my hair,
> My mouth and nose and eyes scantly
> If one came close he might chance to see,

which is certainly what would have befallen "Topsy" had his hair been uncut for a year or two. Burne-Jones once described him affectionately as "this unnaturally and unnecessarily curly being". He did a series of what he called "The Topsy Cartoons", making fun of his curliness and his fatness—for Morris early lost his youthful slimness, and became sturdy and solid.

In his *Life* of Morris, J. W. Mackail says this about that matter:

His hair remained through life of extraordinary beauty, very thick, fine and strong, with a beautiful curl that made it look like exquisitely wrought metal, and with no parting. It was

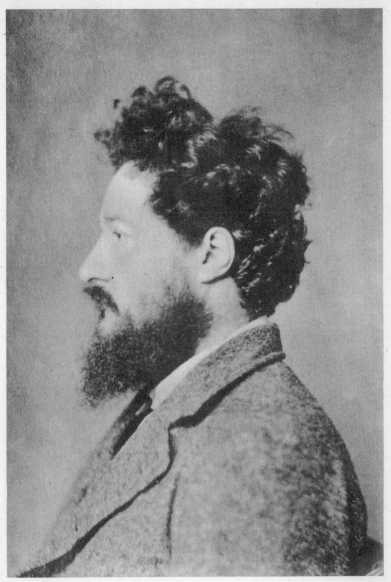

MORRIS IN YOUTH.

so strong that he afterwards used to amuse his children by
letting them take hold of it and lifting them by it off the ground.

Of his eyes, Burne-Jones's wife said that they "always
seemed to me to take in rather than give out".

The picturesqueness of "Topsy's" appearance was
naturally a great boon to his artist friends, and he was often
the model from whom they painted. He did equally well
for Lancelot or one of the Three Kings. From a church
window here and there he still looks down, while in the
Moxon-illustrated Tennyson of 1857, Rossetti drew him—
his friends considered it a very close likeness, though the
rebellious hair is hidden under a cap—as Lancelot gazing
at the Lady of Shallot dead in the barge in which she went
"drifting down to Camelot".

Rossetti not only took Morris for a model—as later
he was to take Morris's romantically lovely wife—but he
shaped the young architect's life with compulsive fingers.
Burne-Jones was completely under the influence; Morris
almost as much so, though, unlike his friend, only for a
time. According to Rossetti, to be a painter was the whole
duty of man, and had Morris been less vigorous his
strenuous efforts to obey this doctrine and yet continue
with his training and career as an architect might easily
have wrecked his health.

Burne-Jones had left Oxford and was working in
Chelsea, and Morris used to work at Street's Oxford office
during the week, and then rush to London to be with Burne-
Jones and Rossetti at the end of each week. He visited
picture shows and fell under the spell of the pre-Raphaelites.
He met Madox Brown and Holman Hunt. He bought,
because of his joy in it, Arthur Hughes' "April Love".

In the autumn of 1856 Street moved his office and
business from Oxford to London, which at once made
things simpler for "Topsy" and Edward Burne-Jones, and
they at once proceeded to set up house together "in the
quaintest room in all London", in Bloomsbury. Architecture

all day for Morris, and painting practically all night. It was small wonder that at this time he took as his motto: "If I can", from that of Jan Van Eyck, "Als ich kann".

But in this instance he found that he couldn't, and by the end of that year he finally gave up architecture as a career, though he never ceased to have a passion for architecture as a study.

So there he was at the age of twenty-three, with a hundred enthusiasms, with no career, and with plenty of money, so that he was not compelled to work for his bread. A dangerous situation for a young man, but, as it happened, not dangerous to William Morris, for idleness was a thing he had no taste for.

II

One of Rossetti's dictums, which he enforced continually on his disciples, was: "If any man has any poetry in him he should paint, for it has all been said and written, and they have scarcely begun to paint it."

But if Rossetti had a powerful personality, so had the young Morris, and he had certain foundations which were unknown to Rossetti. For a while Rossetti succeeded in pushing Morris into the career of a painter—to the quite natural distress of Morris's mother, who must have wondered whether her William was no more than a creature of oscillating moods: first the Church abandoned, and then architecture. Because he was thus pushed, the next year or so, though spent with Burne-Jones in the same pursuit, were not entirely happy. Topsy's temper, so gay and lively, though violent at times, became distinctly moody and irritable. Neither his hand nor his head was occupied in the way his nature really needed.

He and Burne-Jones moved at this time to the rooms in Red Lion Square which ever after were to be linked with

their names. As it proved, these rooms provided an un-
planned opening for Morris's constructive genius. They
were unfurnished, and nothing that could then be bought
was tolerable to the beauty-instructed eyes of these young
artists. And Morris, if not Burne-Jones, needed not only
beauty but a definite solidity. He was so unconsciously
strong that he was very destructive to furniture, unless it
was unusually massive. He had a habit of twisting his legs
round the rungs of a chair, which was in consequence
never the same after he had sat upon it. With the muscles
of his back, as he talked, he would disintegrate the slats of
a chair, and never know he had done it. Chippendale
and Hepplewhite would have shuddered at his very
presence, save for the fact that they were out of fashion
in the 1850's. Mrs. Burne-Jones described how he once
painted a tree in a friend's beautiful garden, "with such
energy that it was long before the grass grew again on the
spot where his chair had stood".

To satisfy all their needs of beauty and solidity it was
obvious that furniture would have to be designed and made
to furnish the rooms at Red Lion Square, and to this end
Morris and Philip Webb proceeded. Massive carpenter-
made furniture began to appear in the empty rooms,
furniture at which Rossetti scoffed joyfully: "Intensely
medieval furniture, tables and chairs like incubi and
succubi."

There was a large round table, "as firm, and as heavy
as a rock", and some chairs "such as Barbarossa might
have sat in". Then a vast settle was designed—this settle
became a "set piece" in the life of the Morris family, it was
not an easy thing to shake off—which had three projecting
cupboards above the long seat. Burne-Jones gives an
amusing account of this famous settle:

There were many scenes with the carpenter, especially I
remember the night when the settle came home. We were
out when it reached the house, but when we came in all the
passage and the staircase were choked with vast blocks of

timber, and there was a scene. I think the measurements had perhaps been given a little wrongly, and that it was bigger altogether than he had ever meant, but set up it was finally, and our studio was one-third less in size.

The mammoth settle roused Rossetti's ribald laughter, but its very size suggested to him that it could have pictures painted on the panels—so thereon was almost at once depicted the Meeting of Dante and Beatrice in Florence and their Meeting in Paradise. Rossetti also painted pictures on the backs of the medieval chairs. There was also a large wardrobe made, which in the following spring of 1857 Burne-Jones decorated with scenes from Chaucer's *Prioress's Tale*. Later this became an important part of the Morris drawing-room at Kelmscott House at Hammersmith, where it stood decoratively at one end of the long room, against the walls hung with Morris's own Strawberry Thief chintz.

This furniture, so massively though light-heartedly made for the rooms at Red Lion Square, was the seed from which sprang the firm of Morris & Company.

Red Lion Square had also another gift to offer in the shape of the young woman, who is known to history as Red Lion Mary. Unlike most of the women associated with these artists, both privately and pictorially, Mary was plain, had no beauty. But that was of no consequence, even in their eyes, for Mary was a person. She was wise and competent. She made the rooms a home for them; she not only cooked and cleaned and mended Topsy and Ned, she took an intelligent interest in what they were doing, read their books, watched them while they were painting. Burne-Jones was always gentle, but Red Lion Mary was sometimes annoyed by Topsy's explosive temper, though she was devoted to him, and proud to feel that he needed her such a lot. She declared that she was "his man Friday".

Morris taught her to embroider, and was gratified to find that she did it quite well—he expected every woman to be able to use the decorative needle, as he could himself. He regarded embroidery as one of the necessary domestic crafts, just as peasant communities have always done.

At a later period Georgiana Burne-Jones said of Morris's knowledge of embroidery that "he taught his wife and me what stitches to use and how to place them: my own experience was that his instructions could not be improved upon and that disaster followed their neglect".

When Red Lion Mary was embroidering Morris's designs for hangings he was always in the utmost impatience to see how they would look, and to hasten that end of his often made Mary with her embroidery frame come into the studio where he was painting, so that he might watch her progress—Morris always had the idea that one piece of time ought to cover two jobs. One day he was at work, and she was sitting quietly embroidering, when Morris suddenly burst out at her: "Mary, be quiet —don't make that insufferable noise."

His work, as Mrs. Burne-Jones who tells the story, comments, was probably going badly.

"No, sir, I won't, sir," said mouse-like Mary.

No wonder Rossetti called her "a most remarkable girl".

12

When the question of decorating the Oxford Union came along, and at Rossetti's demand Burne-Jones and Morris hied them to Oxford for the purpose of applying coloured decoration to new plaster, it meant for Morris leaving Red Lion Square for over a year. When the Union work was finished the spell of Oxford was on him again, and unlike Burne-Jones he did not return to London. Once back in Oxford, and away from the constant overpowering influence of Rossetti, Topsy became his old self again.

He loved the free association with his own friends, but then as always hated formal society. The story is told that being asked with Burne-Jones to a doctor's dinner-party (Morris was apparently under the impression that his host was a donnish doctor, not a medical one) he sent Ned off to do duty for them both, excusing himself on the plea of illness. The doctor, thinking it was a case for professional aid, left his other guests and came round to see what he could do. To their mutual horror Morris was discovered, in a flourishing state of health, dining cheerfully with one of his friends.

The story of the doomed frescoes of the Oxford Union is well known. Less well known are a few sidelights it throws on Morris, given in the words of Burne-Jones, who wrote:

> For the purposes of our drawing we often needed armour, and of a date and design so remote that no examples existed for our use. Therefore Morris, whose knowledge of these things seemed to have been born in him, and who never at any time needed books of reference for anything, set to work to make designs for an ancient kind of helmet called a basinet, and for a great surcoat of ringed mail with a hood of mail and the skirt coming below the knees. These were made for him by a stout little smith who had a forge near the Castle. . . . One afternoon when I was working high up at my picture, I heard a strange bellowing in the building, and turning round to find the cause, saw an unwonted sight. The basinet was being tried on, but the visor, for some reason, would not lift, and I saw Morris embedded in iron, dancing with rage, and roaring inside. The mail coat came in due time, and was so satisfactory to its designer that the first day it came he chose to dine in it. It became him well; he looked very splendid.

While the Oxford Union frescoes were in progress Morris made such lavish decorative use of sunflowers in his bay that Rossetti suggested that he should assist the adjoining artist by painting in a good display of scarlet runners.

Rossetti always enjoyed getting a "rise" out of the uninhibited Morris, as a later story shows, at the time when the Red House was being decorated by this "band of brothers". Entwined with the wall-paintings were some scrolls on which Morris was scribing his motto: "If I can." While his back was turned Rossetti found great satisfaction in writing instead: "As I can't." On discovering this, Topsy's language had to be heard to be believed.

Had the decoration of the Oxford Union been completed, and had the artists known enough about the technical processes of fresco to ensure the permanence of their work, there is no doubt that the scheme would have added another art treasure to Oxford. The colours were of the utmost brilliance. Coventry Patmore, who saw them before they had begun to fade and peel from the walls, described the colours in which they were painted as "sweet, bright, and pure as a cloud in the sunrise", declaring they were "so brilliant as to make the walls look like the margin of an illuminated manuscript".

The subjects of the frescoes were all Arthurian, and as planned Rossetti was to paint Lancelot's Vision of the Sangrail, and he also proposed to do two more, Lancelot found in Guenevere's Chamber, and the Three Knights of the Sangrail. Burne-Jones was to paint the Death of Merlin; Morris, How Sir Palomydes Loved La Belle Iseult; Arthur Hughes, the Death of Arthur; Prinsep, Sir Pelleus and the Lady Ettarde; Pollen, How King Arthur Received his Sword Excalibur from the Lady of the Lake; and Stanhope, Sir Gawaine and the Three Damsels.

Morris, of course, never became a painter in the way that Rossetti tried to force upon him—he became a decorator, an illuminator, but not the creator of easel pictures. He tried hard, but it was not his natural bent. His first picture was somewhat lengthily entitled—these pre-Raphaelite young men gave thought to the "legends" of their pictures— "Sir Tristram after his Illness in the Garden of King Mark's Palace, recognized by the Dog he had given to Iseult."

This was joyfully parodied by his friends, and renamed: "Sudden Indisposition of Sir Tristram in the Garden of King Mark's Palace, recognizable as Collywobbles by the pile of gooseberry skins beside him, remains of the unripe gooseberries devoured by him while he was waiting for Iseult."

Another of Morris's paintings, done in 1858, shows considerable accomplishment in the Pre-Raphaelite manner. It is called simply La Belle Iseult, and shows her in her bed-chamber, standing before a mirror buckling her girdle over a long flowing gown. All the detail is elaborate, and lovingly painted—the half thrown back richly embroidered coverlet of her bed, the decorated chest on which the mirror stands, the delicately diapered cloth on the chest, and the illuminated Missal lying to the side of the mirror, the fine rug at her feet, and the great copper water-jug. Iseult's face has more character than beauty, which in the Rossetti–Burne-Jones circle is a rather refreshing change—she looks both unhappy and cross, which is to say she looks human.

13

The outstanding event in the year 1858 in the life of William Morris is the publication of his first volume of poems, *The Defence of Guenevere*. He had just completed his twenty-fourth year when this volume appeared, yet it contains an epitome of his qualities—all that William Morris was to become is shadowed forth there.

No less a poet than Swinburne wrote of it:

Such things as are in this book are taught and learned in no school but that of instinct. Upon no piece of work in the world was the impress of native character ever more distinctly stamped, more deeply branded. It needed no exceptional acuteness of ear or eye to see or hear that this poet held of none,

"LA BELLE ISEULT"

by William Morris

stole from none, clung to none, as tenant, or as beggar, or as thief. Not yet a master, he was assuredly no longer a pupil.

Certain technical faults, a certain confusion, Swinburne notes, but his praise far outweighs his blame when he goes on to say:

> But where among other and older poets of his time and country is one comparable for perception and experience of tragic truth, of subtle and noble, terrible and piteous things? Where a touch of passion at once so broad and so sure?

The poems in this volume show how Morris's mind had been touched by Malory and by Froissart. There is real passion and extraordinary beauty in the Arthurian poems —the abrupt opening of Guenevere's *Defence* takes the breath with its vibrant quality, half-way between a cry and a blow. But though these poems are fresh and strongly felt, they are in what may be called the tapestry tradition, whereas the poems that derive rather from Froissart than from Malory, like "Sir Peter Harpdon's End", "Concerning Geoffrey Teste Noir", and the grim "Haystack in the Floods", show that Morris realized war had other aspects than that of the tourney, even in the Middle Ages. In spite of his lifelong passion for beauty—which completely escaped any touch of effeminacy owing to the vigour of his nature—there was the need in him for something harsh and stark, which was so completely satisfied when in later years he discovered the Icelandic Sagas, and produced his own greatest work in *Sigurd the Volsung*.

Touches of his later power are seen in this first volume of his poems, and there is something of a Shakespearian poignancy when he makes Alice, Sir Peter Harpdon's wife, cry, when told of her husband's death:

> I am much too young to live,
> Fair God, so let me die.

There are many other things also in this first book of poems; simple-seeming lyrics like "Golden Wings", flowing

as smoothly as water in the manner Morris made his own,
reflecting in this case early memories:

> Midways of a wallèd garden,
>   In the happy poplar land,
>   Did an ancient Castle stand
> With an old knight for a warden.

> Many scarlet bricks there were
>   In its wall, and old grey stone;
>   Over which red apples shone
> At the right time of the year.

> On the bricks the green moss grew,
>   Yellow lichen on the stone,
>   Over which red apples shone;
> Little war that Castle knew.

> Deep green water fill'd the moat,
>   Each side had a red-brick lip
>   Green and mossy with the drip
> Of dew and rain, there was a boat

> Of carven wood, with hangings green,
>   About the stern; it was great bliss
>   For lovers to sit there and kiss
> In the hot summer noons not seen.

> Across the moat the first wet wind
>   In very little ripples went;
>   The way the heavy aspens bent
> Towards it was a thing to mind.

We are already, so many years too early, in the country
of the *Well at the World's End* and the *Water of the Wondrous
Isles*. From that same country comes this:

> There was a lady lived in a hall,
> Large of her eyes and slim and tall;
> And ever she sang from morn to morn,
> *Two red roses across the moon.*

And amid the dreams, and the histories of past lives, and battles long ago, there is the plain and perfect little poem where Morris speaks simply as himself, a thing he did not often do, called "Summer Dawn".

> Pray but one prayer for me 'twixt thy closed lips,
> Think but one thought of me up in the stars.
> The summer night waneth, the morning light slips,
> Faint and grey 'twixt the leaves of the aspen, betwixt the
>   cloud-bars,
> That are patiently waiting there for the dawn:
> Patient and colourless, though Heaven's gold
> Waits to float through them along with the sun.
> Far out in the meadows, above the young corn,
> The heavy elms wait, and restless and cold
> The weary wind rises; the roses are dim;
> Through the long twilight they pray for the dawn,
> Round the lone house in the midst of the corn.
> Speak but one word to me over the corn,
> Over the tender, bow'd locks of the corn.

There is no exaggeration in saying that young William Morris's *Defence of Guenevere* was a remarkable first volume of poetry. But as is the manner of most early volumes of poems it made no particular difference to the year 1858 in which it appeared. Perhaps because of that—though more probably because Morris did not think there was anything particularly difficult or notable about writing poetry—he did not write any more for some time. If Ned Burne-Jones and Rossetti—to whom the volume was dedicated—and a few other of his friends liked his "grinds", which was the group's name for his poetry, he was content. He was engaged on other things, new and exciting things, like tapestry-weaving and his first experiments with dyeing.

14

In the Guenevere volume there is a poem called "Portrait of my Lady", and to Morris personally it was probably the most important poem in the book. From all that is told of him throughout his life it seems that women meant much less to him than his men friends. One of his older friends even said of him in his later years that he knew nothing of the love of women. As a model for the painter, as an inspiration to the poet (the attitude of the Troubadors), he admired them in the abstract. As concrete individuals that "inward eye" of his glanced over them with little lively interest.

There are indications here and there that the sisters and female friends of the men he knew looked at him with some attention and would not have ignored a response on his side. Of all this Morris was apparently completely unconscious. La Belle Iseult, or the Lady of Shalott, or Guenevere, he saw them much more clearly than the girls who fluttered gaily about the streets and gardens of Oxford. But though he thus escaped the small wounds and entanglements of love's wars, his wound when it came was final if not mortal. Small wonder to anyone who reads his description of the "Lady". That the "Praise" was close and accurate, not just a poet lover's rhapsody glorifying into a goddess a very mortal girl, is attested by the actual portraits that were painted of her, and which may still be seen.

This is how she appeared in the eyes of William Morris:

> My lady seems of ivory
> Forehead, straight nose, and cheeks that lie
> Hollow'd a little mournfully,
> *Beata mea Domina!*
>
> Her forehead, overshadow'd much
> By bows of hair, has a wave such
> As God was good to make for me,
> *Beata mea Domina!*

JANE MORRIS BY ROSSETTI.

The next three verses more fully describe her wonderful dark hair, then comes:

> Her great eyes, standing far apart,
> Draw up some memory from her heart,
> And gazed out very mournfully;
>   *Beata mea Domina!*
>
> So beautiful and kind they are,
> But most times looking out afar,
> Waiting for something, not for me,
>   *Beata mea Domina!*
>
> I wonder if the lashes long,
> Are those that do her bright eyes wrong,
> For always half tears seem to be,
>   *Beata mea Domina!*
>
> Lurking below the under lid,
> Darkening the place where they lie hid—
> If they should rise and flow for me!
>   *Beata mea Domina!*
>
> Her full lips being made to kiss,
> Curl'd up and pensive each one is;
> This makes me faint to stand and see.
>   *Beata mea Domina!*

That is not all the poem, but in spite of the rather stiff rapture it shows the close observation of an artist's eye. Morris could not help seeing accurately, even when he was in love. And unlike Pygmalion he had no need to make his dream: she was there, actually walking in the streets of Oxford.

Book Two
MARRIAGE

I

The young woman who inspired that poem was called by the plain and lovely name of Jane Burden. She was so strangely beautiful, though with a melancholy cast of countenance, that she might have walked out of Malory straight into Morris's arms. No wonder he had never looked at other girls if she was his destined type. In these less romantic days, when the demoiselle from faery lands forlorn is no longer admired, it is a little difficult to believe that she really existed as Rossetti painted her—those sad enormous eyes, that deep-curved mouth, that mass (no wonder her long throat was bowed under the weight of it) of heavy waving midnight hair. But she really was like that. There are not only Rossetti's paintings, there are those of other artists—in such a circle such a model could not hope to escape—and there is the cold, unemotional eye of the camera. There is in particular a photograph of her taken in 1866, seated sideways in a wicker chair, wearing a flowing dark silk dress, with wide sleeves turned back with white and embroidery, the whole pose and fall of the drapery enchanting. Her face is turned in profile—showing the lovely jaw-line, the sculptured mouth, the straight nose, the dark brows and eyes, the wings of rich hair lying against her long neck.

In his delightful book of reminiscences, *Time Was*, W. Graham Robertson says of her that she

required to be seen to be believed, and even then she seemed dreamlike. In her habit as she lived did Rossetti paint her over and over again, and all the pictures striking likenesses, many

54

of them most faithful portraits, yet her face is almost invariably looked upon as a figment of a painter's brain, a strange and impossible ideal.

Jane Burden's, he says, was one of the few "World Faces".

No wonder that when young William Morris met this face he was as shattered as was Dante when he met Beatrice. He first saw her at a little theatre in Oxford where he and Burne-Jones had gone for an evening's relaxation after working at the Union frescoes. Jane Burden and her sister were seated exactly behind them, and it can be imagined that the stage that evening did not hold much of their attention. With the directness of young artists they soon managed to introduce themselves, and Morris received permission to paint the face that had swum into his ken.

It is said that after he had tried to paint her for a while, he wrote on his canvas: "I cannot paint you, but I love you", and showed it to her dumbly. It was no long time before they were betrothed, soon after the publication of the *Defence of Guenevere*, wherein was Morris's "Praise" of his Lady.

For a year after his engagement Morris wandered about in a somewhat unsettled manner, visiting France again with some of his Oxford friends, collecting beautiful things —there is a strong suggestion in his life that Jane Burden herself was one of the beautiful things he had "collected" —and finally coming to the conclusion that it was not his destiny to be a painter. That was the third career dropped before he was twenty-five: the Church, architecture, painting. Generally he was in a rather curious frame of mind. He was really growing, but did not know it, and found the process uncomfortable. It probably was also rather uncomfortable for Jane Burden.

She was beginning her part in the life of the great man who was to become her husband—which was to look beautiful, not to share his interests except in a faint feminine way. He did not want a wife who really took part in his work. He could only really share his vital interests with one or two men.

In all the writings and remembrances about William Morris there is curiously little about "Janey". Everyone calls her lovely and kind, but nobody says what she was actually like as a person, unless it be Graham Robertson, who says:

> I fancy that her mystic beauty must sometimes have weighed rather heavily upon her. Her mind was not formed upon the same tragic lines as her face; she was very simple, and could have enjoyed simple pleasures with simple people, but such delights were not for her. She looked like the Delphic Sybil and had to behave as such . . . she seemed to melt from one picture into another, all by Rossetti and all incredibly beautiful.

In 1859, on the 25th of April, William Morris and Jane Burden were married in the ancient church of St. Michael's at Oxford. Dixon, who by this time was in Orders, came from his curacy at Lambeth to unite the two. Burne-Jones and a few of the others were there to see the beautiful bride wedded to their old friend Topsy. The members of the Oxford Brotherhood were all setting forth on their various ways through the world—the idea that they should all pilgrimage in one company had been abandoned, though two or three of them kept in close touch throughout their lives.

2

With marriage the radiating and somewhat wandering lines of Morris's life began to draw together and make a definite pattern. The nucleus of that pattern was a house, a home. Partly through his architectural training, partly through inborn feeling, he was very conscious of houses.

Many people go through life with no more consciousness of houses than as a protection from the weather, a roof under which to sleep. Not so Morris. His early Forest houses were stamped faithfully upon his retentive memory; and though he lived in many other places in between whiles, two houses were quite definitely an integral part of his life—his own first house, the Red House in Kent, which he built for himself, and his last home, Kelmscott Manor by the Thames, which was built for him by the hands of those craftsmen of past time whom he loved and understood so well.

Just as he had found no furniture with which he could live happily in those ugly Victorian days, and had to make his own, so he could not find a house in which to begin married life with his beautiful Janey that in any way suited his ideas. So he decided that he must build one.

There was no difficulty about this, for he had the money to do so, and he had the architect in his own particular friend Philip Webb. The work of Philip Webb was to have a great influence on English domestic architecture in the years to follow, and it was singularly suitable that he began his career with the house—in those days quite outstanding—he built for Morris.

The architect being so perfectly to hand, it only remained to find a parcel of land, and Morris could set out upon one of the most enchanting of human adventures—that of building a house.

The site was found at Upton in Kent, and Rossetti—who had a finger in this pie, as he had in most of Morris's early pies—was convulsed with delight when he discovered that a hollow near by was known locally as "Hog's Hole". Thenceforward that was his name for the lovely Morris home, which was more formally christened Red House, as it was built of rosy brick. In those Victorian days of prevailing stucco, before brick had returned to domestic building, that alone was enough to distinguish the house.

The piece of land that Morris had bought to build upon

was partly planted with an apple orchard. It was set round with blossoming trees that he visioned his home, Janey's beautiful dark head against that background, as if in a Book of Hours, illuminated, with the gold of the sun and the colours of flowers. And his dreams came true— the beauty of his wife was already there, the beauty of his house was soon to rise from its foundations into the Kentish air.

The surrounding country, then unbuilt upon, was of a simple sort, not, says Morris's biographer, "of any remarkable charm: it held something of the sadness of that common English lowland country of which Morris was so fond; but was fertile, well wooded and watered, and interspersed with pleasant orchards and coppices . . . the wide arid heaths of Surrey and the close rich Devonshire valleys were alike distasteful to him; he set his own plain and rather ugly Essex country far before either. But, till he went to live on the Upper Thames, Kent was probably his favourite county."

At any rate it was in Kent that he had chosen to make the first home that was really his own. And as Burne-Jones was to say a year or two later: "Top is slowly making Red House the beautifullest place on earth."

3

The planning of the Red House was as unusual as its building material of brick. It was L-shaped, and its roofs had the medieval charm of a steep pitch, which was emphasized by the turret in the angle which had the fine oaken staircase, and by the enchanting well-house in the courtyard, with its circular, conical, tiled roof, like a witch's hat, the contemplation of which was a joy to all beholders. This well was not only highly decorative but necessary, as there was no water laid on to the house in the Morris days.

THE RED HOUSE, UPTON.

The corridors ran on the inner courtyard walls, so that
the rooms looked outward to the gardens and the bowling-
green, guarded on either side by orchard trees. The place
was very like one of Morris's poems come alive. But in
spite of certain fairy-tale touches it was a solid architectural
house, finely proportioned, and not without severity. All
its ornament was structural, in the true and proper building
tradition.

The plan, unusual at that day, is most attractive, but
the aspect of the house is all wrong according to modern
views, as the principal rooms—dining-room, sitting-room,
drawing-room, and studio—all look north-east, save for a
little glimpse of west which the drawing-room got from
a small oriel window; while the kitchen and pantry look
due west, a bad aspect for both. As there was no reason
in the site for this layout it may have been due to lack of
experience on Webb's part, or to some curious prejudice
of Morris's for looking north—old houses commonly faced
north, as our forefathers believed the south aspect un-
healthy. Anyway, this little group of people were much
more set upon beauty than comfort—though a few of their
visitors were later to complain that the house was cold and
dark—so perhaps they never bothered. Rossetti, writing
to a friend in 1862, said:

> I wish you could see the house which Morris (who has
> money) has built for himself in Kent. It is a most noble work
> in every way, and more a poem than a house, such as any-
> thing else could lead you to conceive, but an admirable place
> to live in too.

The front door and entrance-hall were also to the north,
and over the door was carved

Dominus custodiet Exitum
Tuum et introitum Tuum

Inside, the Red House had a drawing-room on the first
floor, with an oriel window and an open roof, which Morris

enthusiastically declared he was going to make the most beautiful room in England. His own gifts and those of his friends were spent in decorating it, and the history of the Red House always remained a joyful memory in the minds of these friends; they were proving with their own hands the truth of Topsy's saying: "Art is the result of man's joy in his labour."

The famous painted settle from Red Lion Square was set up in the drawing-room, and by means of a ladder at the side and a little door in the wall behind it was designed to turn the massive overhanging top into a minstrels' gallery, which shows what children they were at heart and also the excessive solidity of their furniture. In the dining-room there was a sideboard (if such a commonplace name may be applied to such a piece of furniture) designed by Morris, of an enchanting Gothic quality, with a roof of three gables and a kind of open gallery for dishes—it is much more like a Tudor cottage than a sideboard! The same dining-room has a very beautiful and severely plain brick fireplace—a startling innovation in that day of all the horrors of white marble, ornate cast iron, and dreadful coloured tiles. In the hall was another Gothic and massive clothes-press and bench combined, the panels of which Rossetti partly painted, but did not complete.

As a wedding gift Burne-Jones made for Morris and his bride a richly painted cupboard on which was depicted Chaucer's tale of Little Saint Hugh of Lincoln:

> This litel child, his litel book lernynge,
> As he sat in the scole at his prymer,
> He Alma redemptoris herde synge,
> As children larned hive antiphoner;
> And, as he dorste, he drough hym ner and ner,
> And herkned ay the wordes and the noote,
> Til he the firste vers koude al by rote.

The painted panels are gloriously crowded with figures, angels, Our Lady, Chaucer himself with his ink-horn and quill, and in the background the walls and towers of Lincoln.

Philip Webb not only designed the Red House, but also a good deal of the needed furniture to complete it. There was a great oak dining-table which he designed, a noble piece of timberwork, and many other necessary furnishings, as well as superb copper candlesticks and glass and many other smaller household things. Morris had the curious idea —for that day—that things of daily household use should be beautiful and should be used, not kept in glass-fronted show cabinets. He always lived up to his own precept: "Have nothing in your houses that you do not know to be useful, or believe to be beautiful."

All these enthusiastic young people were imbued with this desire, and with their own hands they carried it out whenever it was possible. The men decorated the walls with paintings; the women adorned the hangings and cushions with embroidery, and if at first they were not so skilled in this craft as Birdalone in *The Water of the Wondrous Isles*, they soon became so. One trouble they were faced with was the lack at that time of any beautiful materials for their work; the least objectionable fabric they could find to embroider upon was coarse serge.

In her *Memorials* of her husband Georgiana Burne-Jones gives an enchanting account of these early days at Red House, full of youth and happiness and the joy of making beautiful things which is the natural heritage of man. "Oh, how happy we were, Janey and I," she says, "busy in the morning with needlework or wood-engraving, and in the afternoon driving to explore the country round with the help of a map of Kent."

In the intervals of painting and decorating—Burne-Jones planned some pictures from the "Tale of Sir Devregaunt" in tempera for the drawing-room—the men played bowls, and Morris planned his garden. He had ideas about that, as he had ideas about everything else, though he was not a man who actually spent large portions of his days in digging: the processes of gardening were a little slow for his forward-marching mind. But he *knew* about gardening, as he knew about medieval armour and other things, and the results were delightful, as Mrs. Burne-Jones describes them:

> Many flowering creepers had been planted against the walls of the house from the earliest possible time, so that there was no look of raw newness about it, and the garden, beautiful before by the apple-trees, quickly took shape. In front of the house it was spaced formally into fair little square gardens making a big square together; each of the smaller squares had a wattled fence round it with an opening by which one entered, and all over the fence roses grew thickly. The stable, with stalls for two horses, stood in one corner of the garden, end on to the road, and had a kind of younger-brother look to the house. The deep porches . . . were at the front and back of the house, the one at the back was practically a small garden-room. There was a solid table in it, painted red, and fixed to the wall was a bench where we sat and talked and looked out into the Well-Court, of which two sides were formed by the house and the other two by a tall rose-trellis. This little court, with its beautiful high-roofed brick well in the centre summed up the feeling of the whole place.

And Morris's biographer gives this little picture of that garden:

> Red House garden, with its long grass walks, its mid-summer lilies and autumn sunflowers, its wattled rose-trellises enclosing richly flowered square garden plots, was then as unique as the house it surrounded . . . apples fell in at the windows as they stood open on hot summer nights.

It must not be forgotten that this half medieval, half cottage garden that Morris made came before the days of garden enlightenment; it belonged to the days of "bedding-out", when the blue lobelia, the yellow calceolaria, and the scarlet geranium were clashing triumphantly in all respectable Victorian gardens.

The pursuit of beauty within doors and without was tempered by riotous horseplay and fun, of which Morris himself was continually the far from meek victim. One of the jokes was to send him to Coventry and refuse to communicate with him save through his wife. They played slightly alarming games of hide-and-seek through the house in the dark. More comfortably they sang old English songs in the evening by the fire. They told riddles, and great joy was caused when one of them asked:

"Who killed his brother Cain?"

Morris, proud of his Biblical knowledge, answered: "Abel, of course."

He laughed with the rest at his mistake and the easy way he had fallen into the trap, and was so pleased about it that he tried the trick on someone else, and told of its success with pride.

"I asked him", he said, "who killed his brother Abel? and when of course he said 'Cain', I said 'Hah! I knew you'd say that—everyone says it!'"

His triumphant face, as Georgiana Burne-Jones said, made them laugh again, "more than before".

Topsy was very good fun to tease, he was so explosive, and the more he roared at them and shook his leonine head the more they loved him.

4

Since their marriage, after a six weeks' honeymoon abroad, Morris and his wife had dwelt in Great Ormond Street while the Red House was being built. It was not till the end of the summer of 1860 that they were able to move to their own home and begin the great adventure of adorning it according to their wishes. Morris's schemes were big; he meant the decorating and furnishing of his house to be a matter of years, not a hurried job of a few weeks. He had the leisure and vision of the medieval mind, and at the end of five years the house was still growing in beauty.

3*

The Red House was really the origin of the firm of Morris & Company. At the beginning there were other names in the title, but they gradually dropped out: for Morris was from the start the chief figure, the man who supplied the money, who designed and planned and adventured down new paths and embarked on untried crafts. It was really the slightly nebulous "brotherhood" taking a firmer commercial shape and calling itself in the circular issued in 1861: "Morris, Marshall, Faulkner & Co. Fine Art Workmen in Painting, Carving, Furniture and Metals." They declared that they "have felt more than most people the want of some one place where they could either obtain or get produced work of a genuine and beautiful character".

The first workshop and showroom was at 8 Red Lion Square.

The taste for Morris chintzes, tapestries, and wallpapers is in abeyance in these days, and if it existed could not be satisfied, as the firm is no longer in existence. But the people who now feel that Morris's work was over-decorated and elaborate do not realize, even in imagination, the domestic horrors of the British home round about the 1860's—the niggling monstrosities in furniture and design, the shocking colours; costliness, not beauty, ornateness, not line, being the only criterion of value then.

The work and the influence of the firm of Morris and Company on English interior decoration, and abroad also, was simply revolutionary. And in spite of the modern dislike or distrust of pattern—fully justified when, as is too often the case, it is feeble or aggravating pattern—those who have lived for years with a Morris hanging know how satisfactory it is. Morris's sense of design was so instinctive and good that he knew how to make a pattern at once soothing and stimulating—the lines flow, and it is as pleasant and natural to the eye as a wall draped with living verdure, or a meadow full of field flowers. The delicate interlacing design of the "Willow Bough" wallpaper, the magnificence

of the "Pomegranate", and the enchanting stiffness of the
"Daisy" are each in their different ways delightful. He
designed altogether nearly fourscore wallpapers, which the
firm produced by wood-block printing in the traditional
manner, with tempera colours.

In his designs for cotton, linen, silk, and wool fabrics
Morris showed the same flowing invention and grace; he
could use the bold architectural shapes of the acanthus
leaf, or the humble little eyebright equally well. That
little "Eyebright" cotton on an indigo ground was a thing
of many uses, from a curtain or a cushion cover for a cottage
room, to a child's frock. And there were so many other
chintzes; the "Strawberry Thief" in particular enchanted
several generations. There is definitely less gaiety and
colour in the world because these chintzes of William
Morris's are no longer to be had.

It is doubtful if there ever has been a finer pattern-
designer than he was, even in the glowing Middle Ages.
He did it as naturally as he breathed. He had the art of
covering a surface with effortless design, so flowing that it
looked as if the wind moved among the leaf and flower
forms, so gracious that the "repeat" of the pattern never
assaulted the eye. He could do this equally well with large
or small forms, though perhaps the large was more natural
to the natural boldness of his mind.

Of course the range of the new firm was not confined
to wallpapers and fabrics, in fact it did not even begin with
them. The Anglo-Catholic revival called for a lot of church
decoration in something different from the "ecclesiastical
outfitter" style. Stained glass, painted decoration, tapestries, church embroidery, all came within the work of
Morris & Company. Burne-Jones and Madox Brown
designed many windows for the firm, including those for
St. Martin's, Scarborough, and St. Michael's, Brighton,
which Bodley was then building. The chancel roof of that
church was painted by Morris, Faulkner, and Philip Webb
with their own hands. Another church at Brighton—St.

Paul's—has Morris as a king and Swinburne as a shepherd in one of the windows. Rottingdean's little old church has a set of Burne-Jones–Morris windows, and Rye Church has the last window—that of the Three Kings at Bethlehem —made by those two friends together.

This firm, which was to grow and spread—contrary to all that might have been expected from its amateur status and lack of business experience, Faulkner being the only member who had any knowledge of finance—was started on a capital of one hundred pounds. This sum of money was lent by Morris's mother, without any security except her belief in her son. It is refreshingly contrary to all the normal methods. But the people who were running that show were not business men—they were artists and craftsmen, whose first object was not profit but the making of honest and beautiful things. Of course the firm, which ultimately bore his sole name, got through its teething troubles because Morris was always there to put his hand in his pocket when money ran short, as it constantly and inevitably did. He did this so unfailingly and so generously that there was a period when he found himself very straitened for his own needs—distinctly a new experience to him. He had always been accustomed to a liberal supply and had always used it with generous freedom, but the claims of the firm, and the reduction of the yields of the family copper mine from which his comfortable income largely came, made him realize that there was a possibility that money might run short. But his financial support of the business never faltered in the early anxious years when work was sometimes carried on at an actual loss. That he maintained the business almost unaided through so crucial a period was due, says Mackail, "to a persistency, a sagacity, an unweariable industry, for which he has seldom received adequate credit".

Faulkner, who may be regarded as the business head of the concern in so far as it had one, wrote an amusing account of the firm's proceedings:

It has meetings once or twice a fortnight which have rather the character of a meeting of the "Jolly Masons" or the jolly something else's than of a meeting to discuss business. Beginning at 8 for 9 p.m. they open with the relation of anecdotes which have been culled by members of the firm since the last meeting—this store having been exhausted, Topsy and Brown will perhaps discuss the relative merits of the art of the thirteenth and fifteenth century, and then perhaps after a few more anecdotes, business matters will come up about 10 or 11 o'clock.

Morris's wife and Burne-Jones's wife, Janey and Georgie, with other women working under their direction, made embroidered hangings for the firm, and William De Morgan made tiles—those lovely tiles for which he was famous long before he made a second reputation as an enchanting and somewhat Dickensian kind of novelist, with those endlessly long stories in which there is not a word too much. One of these novels, *Alice-for-Short*, was dedicated to the memory of Morris and Burne-Jones, who were both dead then.

Every new craft that was started by the firm, every new thing attempted, was started and attempted by Morris. Even the embroidered hangings on coarse serge obtained from a Yorkshire woollen manufacturer, worked in bright wools, was tried by Morris. "Top has taken to worsted work", said Rossetti rather scornfully, for an artist to him meant a painter and nothing else. But Top took to everything, and was as eager to see what other men had achieved, as to survey his own work. William De Morgan has described how he came pounding into his kiln, shouting to see the new tile, or the new lustre pot. All his life he was continually emphasizing how the workman should have joy in his work and not look for it only in his recreation. Work to him was always joy, but in these early years he had not yet come to see how many men have to work at jobs in which there is no possibility of joy. When he realized this he did not just shrug his shoulders, declare it was a pity, and continue with his own beautiful handicrafts. That is one reason why he is a much bigger figure, a much bigger human being, than all the artists among whom his life was spent.

5

While the firm was staggering on to its business feet, the Red House, from which the firm had sprung, was flourishing as a centre of beauty and work and happiness. Morris and his wife and Burne-Jones and his were there continually together, full of schemes and plans. Everybody worked hard at something, and they laughed as they worked because they were enjoying themselves so much, and because Topsy was so ridiculous and so splendid and so delightfully easy to tease. One visitor there said that "there was so much to do in the way of playing bowls and smoking pipes that the day passed without having time to do anything".

Between working at the adorning of the Red House— and work they did, all the usual decorators' work being done with their own hands, not simply designed by them —and playing bowls and talking the moon down the sky, Morris and his friends drove about the Kentish countryside in a carriage Morris had built to his orders, of a semi-Chaucerian design, with leather curtains.

Morris himself was so happy at this time in his chosen setting and with his chosen friends—sometimes there were so many staying there that they had to sleep on the floor of the dining-room—that one of his friends was driven to the declaration: "I grieve to say he has only kicked one pannel out of a door for this twelvemonth past." Sign of an almost unnatural tranquillity on the part of Topsy.

To crown this content Morris's first daughter was born, and christened Jane after her mother and Alice after her father's youngest sister. In the following year Jane Alice had a sister who was christened Mary, but known as May; no Arthurian names like Ettarde or Iseult were chosen. These two daughters completed the quartet of William Morris's family.

But as might almost have been foreseen the Red House days were too perfect, too much as if they were happening in *News From Nowhere*, to endure. The very considerable cost of the building and adorning of the house itself, the increasing expense of the two children, the responsibilities of the firm, and the dwindling of returns of the copper mine, brought Morris down to earth with something of a bump. There were other contributory causes as well. The business, which was expanding though not yet fully paying its way, required larger premises and workshops than it had in Red Lion Square.

This need, and the equal need of Morris and Burne-Jones of being within reach of each other, suggested a superb scheme; the Red House should be added to by the addition of another wing in which the Burne-Joneses were to live, with their own quite separate entrance and quarters; while land near by was to be purchased on which to establish the workshops. This plan would have suited everybody marvellously, but a little plague of sickness put an end to it.

In the September of 1864 the Morris family, the Burne-Joneses and the Faulkners, went for a seaside holiday to Littlehampton on the Sussex coast, then a small and simple place. Burne-Jones's small son Philip and Miss Faulkner both caught scarlet fever there, and a little later Georgiana Burne-Jones caught it from nursing her little boy, and nearly died. About the same time Morris was laid low with rheumatic fever, and for a time was badly crippled. To his robust health and energetic nature this was a sad blow. When he realized that because of health and all the other difficulties the cherished plan of a communal home and workshop must be given up, he wrote a sad letter to Burne-Jones, heading it "In bed, Red House", admitting that he had wept a little with disappointment, but going on: "I am only thirty years old; I shan't always have the rheumatics, and we shall have lots of jolly years of invention and lustre plates together I hope."

From these troubles one plain fact emerged. The Red House scheme was a dream which would have to be abandoned. Instead of bringing the business to his country home Morris would have to go and "live over the shop", in what after all was but a return to the medieval manner in the days—the somewhat mythical days—when he saw London as "small and white and clean".

It was a hard decision, the one that was finally come to, that of giving up the Red House altogether, but rheumatic fever is not a trifling illness; the Red House, though so beautiful, was cold, which was not surprising with its northern aspect, and the journey to the nearest railway station was very bleak and exposed.

So Morris, who believed in doing things thoroughly, made up his mind to part with it, to sell it. Some of the furniture had to be sold with the house—the furniture made with such joy, the "incubi and succubi"—as it was simply too unwieldly to be moved, it needed a house built round it.

Morris never went again to the Red House after he had parted from it; he felt he could not bear to see it again, which is the measure of how dear it had been to him. There his married life had flowered, his two daughters had been born; there his friends and he had made a world of their own; a not quite real world, perhaps, but one in which there had been love and laughter and fellowship, hard work and beauty and youth. To leave Red House for London was to go from dream to reality, from fellowship to a fight—which it is true was yet in the future—and from a questing youth to an assured achievement. But at least in Morris's case the plain prose of life had begun with a magnificent initial letter.

Book Three

MATURITY

I

After Red House there was only one house that greatly
mattered in Morris's grown-up life, and that was Kelmscott
Manor. But he was to have a few wanderings and wayside
homes before he found it. With his passion for beauty and
facility in creating it, he was never content to leave any
place in which he dwelt unadorned. He cared little for
bodily comfort—if you sat in chairs that might have been
used by knights of the Round Table you were not expected
to grumble because they were uncomfortable and too heavy
to move—but he cared a great deal for the satisfaction of
the eye by shape and colour. Which was all in harmony
with pre-Raphaelite ideas and ideals. In that delicious
book, *Three Houses*, the granddaughter of Burne-Jones,
Angela Thirkell, describes some of the furnishings of North
End House, Rottingdean, where she used to visit her
grandparents when she was a child:

"As I look back", she says,

on the furniture of my grandparents' two houses I marvel
chiefly at the entire lack of comfort which the Pre-Raphaelite
Brotherhood succeeded in creating for itself. It was not, I
think, so much that they actively despised comfort, as that the
word conveyed absolutely nothing to them whatever. I can
truthfully say that neither at North End Road nor at North
End House was there a single chair that invited to repose . . .
The sofas at Rottingdean were simply long low tables with a
little balustrade round two, or sometimes three sides, made of
plain oak or some inferior wood painted white. There was a
slight concession to human frailty in the addition of rigidly
hard squabs covered with chintz or blue linen, and when to
these my grandmother had added a small bolster apparently

71

made of concrete, and two or three thin unyielding cushions, she almost blamed herself for wallowing in undeserved luxury . . . As for Pre-Raphaelite beds, it can only have been the physical vigour and perfect health of their original designers that made them believe their work was fit to sleep in.

These furnishings of North End House were of course largely supplied by Morris & Company, and therefore approved by him as well as by the Burne-Joneses, who had such a very austere idea of comfort.

To Morris it was inevitably a sad change from the Red House in its apple orchard to anything that London could offer. Queen Square, Bloomsbury, to which the Morris family and the Morris firm moved simultaneously in the autumn of 1865, had a certain dignity and faded flavour of Queen Anne, which was not, however, a period that architecturally or artistically or for its literature had any appeal to Morris. But No. 26 Queen Square had many practical advantages in its capacity to house a family and house a business under one and the same roof. A large ballroom had once been built at the end of the yard and it made an admirable workshop. In the long corridor that led to the old ballroom the glass-painters worked, and there was a kiln. Other workshops were set up in the buildings off the small court at the back, while the ground floor provided offices and showrooms.

Up above all this industry the family dwelt, in rooms that were made as bright and gay as possible with white-wash and white paint, lovely embroidered hangings and cushions, and painted furniture. Here Morris settled down to work, with the content that work always brought him, but his heart never cleaved to a house again as it had cleaved to Red House, till he found Kelmscott Manor on the Upper Thames.

Nevertheless, Queen Square had undoubted attractions. There was a fine garden-square, with immense plane-trees, where the two little Morris girls spent much of their time.

Needless to say they also haunted the workshops to watch what was going on there whenever they got the chance; always interesting and exciting things were being done, and their young father was the centre of it all.

May Morris, in her Introduction to the third volume of her father's *Collected Works* recalls these Queen Square days with nostalgic grace. She remembers the curly scrolls that used to be perpetually about the house, galley-proofs, and wondering why they often made her father so angry. She also recalls how in the evenings "there sometimes appeared a gloriously, mysteriously shining object, behind which he would work with bright cutting tools on a little block of wood, which sat on a plump leather cushion". He was cutting the wood blocks to illustrate one of his poems.

Then she gives this charming "interior":

> I can well remember the look of the stately five-windowed room, with the long oak table laid for one of these dinners. What specially attracted my attention was not the old silver and blue china, but the greenish glass of delicate shapes, designed by Philip Webb, and made for the firm by Messrs. Powell at the Whitefriars Glass-works. This gleamed like air-bubbles in the quiet candle-light and was reflected far away in the little mirrors set in the chimney-piece, where the room lengthened itself into an endless pleasant mystery at once friendly and alluring to us children.

And amid this gracious scene moved lovely Jane Morris "in soft silk gowns". There is more than a touch of fairy-tale about the early Morris household.

At the lower end of the Square lived the Faulkners—always such faithful friends of Topsy's—at No. 35, and the long upstairs drawing-room "had a delicious country atmosphere of freshness and roses about it".

Philip Webb was also within reach at his chambers in Gray's Inn. The Burne-Jones family were at this time in Kensington, and it became the custom that these close friends and fellow workers should dine together, with their wives, once a week at Queen Square in the long room with its solid oak table and the candles glimmering on the green glass and the old silver. These regular meetings of the two men were never entirely given up, though later on when the Burne-Joneses had moved to the Grange at Fulham they were changed to Morris breakfasting there on Sunday mornings. But before this the two wives ceased to take part in the weekly dinners at Queen Square, as Jane Morris fell out of health and was not able to do a great deal.

2

It is not planned here to tell in detail the story of the firm of Morris & Company, except in so far as it affected the activities of William Morris himself, which of course it did greatly. From the beginning until his death he was the moving spirit—as in the absurd child's story, both the Push-you and the Pull-you. His almost volcanic energies were poured into the firm, and if there was a new craft to be experimented with, a new pie to be made, Morris was trying it and making it. But he was also a great many other things than the leading spirit of the Morris business. He was a poet, a teller of prose tales in a style he invented for himself, so long and leisurely and detailed that it might seem those tales were enough to fill any man's time; more than this he was to become an active working socialist and preacher at street corners; and finally he was to be the creator of the great Kelmscott Press.

After the publication of his first volume of poems, *The Defence of Guenevere*, Morris left poetry alone for a while to devote himself to building a house and building a business. But after the move to Queen Square the poetic stream burst up from the depths again, and he published his second volume of poems, *The Life and Death of Jason*.

In the course of his poetic life Morris told many Greek

legends, but his own mind was not by nature Greek and classic, it was medieval and Gothic, and his setting and backgrounds are much more Chaucerian than Hellenic. He liked the Greek stories, he felt they were great stories, but he wanted to dress them in his own way, and he did. He was fortunate, too, in that people liked his manner of doing it. The *Guenevere* volume had only attracted the notice of a small circle, but *Jason* was a success; its vigorous beauty let a little air into the rather close literary atmosphere of that time. It was published in 1867, and Morris was thirty-four years old when it appeared.

This long poem of *The Life and Death of Jason* showed that Morris possessed a natural gift of narrative. He was fresh and tireless, he told the tale as if he himself had been there and seen everything which he described. His gift of seeing and describing was indeed part of his gift of pattern-designing. There are times in his later work, in parts of the *Earthly Paradise* for instance, when the embroidery is almost too much for the fabric, when it weights it so that it drags; it is the inherited Pre-Raphaelite taint of "too much": too much beauty, too much love, too much languor, too much everything, so that the soul sickens for plain bread, cold water, and a little cheerfulness. Morris's personality was free of this vice, but his poetry suffered from it on occasion, and a too-prolonged reading of some of his poems can cause an exhaustion that almost produces physical faintness; probably the very young are immune from this, for the days of youth are so long.

The Life and Death of Jason was originally intended to fit into the scheme of the *Earthly Paradise*, but it became too extensive, and was completed and published separately. Perhaps in consequence it does not suffer from the weariness of those ancient mariners fleeing from the Plague and searching for a terrestrial paradise. *Jason* is a poem full of lovely things, as when the lovers are fleeing together and they reach the silent quayside where the *Argo* is moored, Medea says the following to Jason:

O love, turn round, and note the goodlihead
My father's palace shows beneath the stars.
Bethink there of the men grown old in wars
Who do my bidding; what delights I have,
How many ladies lie in wait to serve
My life from toil and carefulness, and think
How sweet a cup I have been used to drink,
And how I cast it to the ground for thee.
Upon the day thou weariest of me,
I wish that thou might somewhat think of this,
And twixt thy new-found kisses, and the bliss
Of something sweeter than thine old delight,
Remember thou a little of this night
Of marvels, and this starlit, silent place,
And these two lovers standing face to face.

And when what Medea had bodingly foreseen, when the
day has come that Jason wearies of her and Medea thinks
upon her tragic vengeance, Morris rises to almost Shakespearian heights in the words he puts into her mouth:

But ye—shall I behold you when leaves fall,
In some sad evening of the autumn-tide?
Or shall I have you sitting by my side
Amidst the feast, so that folk stare and say,
Sure the grey wolf has seen the queen to-day?

And most poignant of all:

Must I bethink me of the upturned sods,
And hear a voice say: "Mother, wilt thou come
And see us resting in our new-made home,
Since thou wert used to make us lie full soft,
Smoothing our pillows many a time and oft? . . .
Thy hands would bathe us when we were thine own,
Now doth the rain wash every shining bone."

To those who read such lines for the first time it was
obvious that England had a new poet, though what the
rest of his work was to be, what place he was to hold, it
was plainly impossible for the readers and critics of 1867
to know.

It was clear that to Morris narrative poetry came as naturally as to his master, Chaucer. And in his next published work, the *Earthly Paradise*, he planned a scheme on the Chaucerian model, in which he could tell any tale he chose, whether Greek or medieval, or from the Northern Sagas, which were already laying their spell upon him, without irrelevance or necessity to link them to each other. The only needed link was the period of the fourteenth century, in which the men who told these stories to each other were supposed to be living, all of them under the dread of the Black Death. It was a good scheme, for it enabled Morris quite naturally and rightly to move in the Middle Ages even when telling a Greek story—to see things, as was his instinct, from the angle of a fourteenth-century mind, which would not in the least be concerned with historical anachronisms, the fear of which has so painfully cramped the style of many writers after Chaucer's day.

Morris in his attitude to his own poetry was refreshingly simple. He had a great gift; certain of his lyrics and shorter poems and at least one of his long narrative poems are worthy to rank with anything in the *corpus* of English poetry short of the topmost heights.

The poet of that time—the Wordsworthian simplicities being a little out of the fashion—was expected to pose, to be peculiar: to be wrapped in Olympian glooms like Tennyson, to droop in a hot-house atmosphere like Swinburne, to be strange and slightly sinister like Dante Gabriel Rossetti. But Morris would have nothing of this. He took the opposite attitude to a slightly absurd extent when he said with his usual vigour, "That talk of inspiration is sheer nonsense. I may tell you that flat. There is no such thing; it is a mere matter of craftsmanship."

Which, like a great many other sweeping statements, is not true. But it was true for Morris, and fitted with his other well-known pronouncements: "If this is poetry, it's very easy to do", and "If a chap can't compose an epic poem while he's weaving tapestry, he'd better shut up, he'll never do any good at all."

But there are many chaps who can weave tapestry; not so many who can compose an epic. Morris's mind was so vital and richly stored that he, like the spider, could endlessly draw the threads out of himself. He was among those who are natural creators. He also had that generous kind of simplicity which believed that what he could do anybody else could do, if they wanted to do it. His brain worked as fast as his hands; he could compose seven hundred lines of poetry in a day. The common opinion is that such facility means inferior quality, but water is not necessarily less pure because it flows in abundance. There is such a thing as God's plenty, as shown in the flowing ease with which Bach and Handel wrote their music. Morris had that quality, though admittedly on a much less high spiritual plane. His firm, clear, unmannered handwriting—though now and again he would pause to draw a little flower-sprig on his manuscript—shows how straightforward he was about it all. None of the crabbed agonies of many poets. Here is, we are fain to believe, the true Chaucerian manner and carriage of the pen, even if the matter lacks the rich humanity, humour, pity, of the *Canterbury Tales*.

The whole cycle of the stories of the *Earthly Paradise* is a very spacious one, beginning with a Prologue and ending with an Epilogue, and in between is "The Story of Theseus", "The Son of Crœsus", "Cupid and Psyche", "The King's Treasure-House", "Orpheus and Eurydice", "Pygmalion", "Atalanta's Race", "The Doom of King Acrisius", "Rhodope", "The Dolphin and the Lovers", "The Fortunes of Gygis", "Bellerophon", "The Watching of the Falcon", "The Lady of the Land", "The Hill of Venus", "The Seven Sleepers", "The Man Who Never Laughed Again", "The Palace East of the Sun", "The Queen of the North", "The Story of Dorothea", "The Writing on the Image", "The Proud King", "The Ring

Given to Venus", "The Man Born to be King". Twenty-four stories, two for each month of the year. In between each couple of tales there is a poem for each of the twelve months, beginning with March, and these poems of the months are among some of the loveliest things Morris ever wrote. The stories come from all over the world, but these month poems do not belong to Greece or France or Scandinavia, or any other part of the world; they belong to England; they describe and adore the land in which Morris was born and died.

The opening stanzas of the long narrative Prologue to the *Earthly Paradise* are among Morris's best-known lines:

> Forget six counties overhung with smoke,
> Forget the snorting steam and piston stroke,
> Forget the spreading of the hideous town;
> Think rather of the pack-horse on the down,
> And dream of London, small and white and clean,
> The clear Thames bordered by its gardens green;
> Think, that below bridge the green lapping waves
> Smite some few keels that bear Levantine staves,
> Cut from the yew wood on the burnt up hill,
> And pointed jars that Greek hands toiled to fill,
> And treasured scanty spice from some far sea,
> Florence gold cloth, and Ypres napery,
> And cloth of Bruges, and hogsheads of Guienne;
> While nigh the thronged wharf Geoffrey Chaucer's pen
> Moves over bills of lading——

3

While Morris was working on the *Earthly Paradise* he was also engaged upon his ordinary jobs, for it was against all his instincts to make a fuss about being a poet, even when he was at work upon a poem of such magnitude. Years later he was to say:

Waiting for inspiration, rushing things in reliance on inspiration, and all the rest of it, are a lazy man's habits. Get the bones of the work well into your head, and the tools well into your hand, and get on with the job, and the inspiration will come to you—if you are worth a tinker's damn as an artist, that is!

That was his general method, whether it was a question of writing an epic or designing a chintz.

For part of the summer of 1867 the Morris family and the Burne-Jones family and the Faulkners were all together at Oxford, and while they were there Topsy used to read aloud to his friends in the evening what he had written of his *Earthly Paradise* during the day.

It was a golden summer, and they used to make river excursions together and explore the regions of the Upper Thames, feeling the "desire that rippling water gives to youthful hearts to wander anywhere". They discovered the waters of the Windrush and the meadows by the Evenlode—names which Morris was later to link with his work. The beauty of these days and these scenes got into the great poem he was writing. In the "June" prelude he says:

> O June, O June, that we desired so
> Wilt thou not make us happy on this day?
> Across the river thy soft breezes blow
> Sweet with the scent of bean fields far away,
> Above our heads rustle the aspens grey
> Calm is the sky with harmless clouds beset,
> No thought of storm the morning vexes yet.
>
> See, we have left our hopes and fears behind
> To give our very hearts up unto thee;
> What better place than this then could we find
> By this sweet stream that knows not of the sea,
> That guesses not the city's misery,
> This little stream whose hamlets scarce have names,
> This far-off, lonely mother of the Thames?

Another river journey is reflected in the "August" verses:

> Across the gap made by our English hinds,
> Amidst the Roman's handiwork, behold
> Far-off the long-roofed church; the shepherd binds
> The withy round the hurdles of his fold
> Down in the fosse the river fed of old,
> That through long lapse of time has grown to be
> The little grassy valley that you see.
>
> Rest here awhile, not yet the eve is still,
> The bees are wandering yet, and you may hear
> The barley mowers on the trenchèd hill,
> The sheep-bells, and the restless changing weir,
> All little sounds made musical and clear
> Beneath the sky that burning August gives,
> While yet the thought of glorious summer lives.

Such poems are essentially English. They have that touch of nostalgic sadness most English poets betray when they write of summer, knowing as they do how brief and uncertain is the glory of an English summer's day. It is the same thing, in a lesser degree, that Morris felt so strongly about death; he felt pressingly at times throughout the years how each brief life awaited that Comer whom none can stay. He rarely reached the serenity of Jeremy Taylor's attitude: "Death is the same harmless thing that a poor shepherd suffered yesterday."

Morris was very English in his outlook, even though it was the outlook of an Englishman of a much earlier day, and in spite of his passion for French Gothic architecture and the French scene—he never really cared for Italy in his bones—he was fundamentally an Englishman. His late-discovered and half-terrified love for Iceland and the Icelandic Sagas was in a sense but a heightening of his Englishness. It was the same voice that spoke to him as a boy from Silbury Hill and the stones of Avebury, that spoke to him from the dark hills of Iceland, calling him away from his love of gold and colours and silken textures, from

his *Earthly Paradise*, to the stark histories and the cruel
cold of the North, to the vision of Gudrun at the end when

> She turned, until her sightless eyes did gaze
> As though the walls, the hills, must melt away,
> And show her Herdholt in the twilight grey;
> She cried, with tremulous voice, and eyes grown wet
> For the last time, what e'er should happen yet,
> With hands stretched out for all that she had lost:
> "I did the worst to him I loved the most."

There was a warm south side to William Morris. There
was also a marked north side as well.

4

With the completion of the *Earthly Paradise* a new name
comes into the story of Morris's life, that of F. S. Ellis, who
was a dealer in manuscripts and rare books, and was
also a publisher in a quiet way. In those days his shop was
in King Street, Covent Garden, and later he moved to
charming old bow-windowed premises in Bond Street.

Morris had been a customer of Ellis's before there had
arisen any question of publishing; he bought from him a
work of Boccaccio of 1473, illustrated with woodcuts.
Before he quite decided to give the price asked he brought
a "pale and fragile-looking young man", who was Burne-
Jones, to look at it.

When his *Jason* came out Morris gave a copy to Ellis,
and eventually it was Ellis who published the *Earthly
Paradise*, which first appeared in parts.

This association was to prove of the happiest nature, and
F. S. Ellis became a lifelong friend of Morris and was one
of his executors.

"How much I owe of the bright side of life to him I
cannot reckon", Ellis wrote to Morris's biographer:

He was the very soul of honour, truthfulness, and justice. Not only would he never deviate from the truth, but in thinking carefully over the matter I do not remember him ever to have made plausible excuses for doing or not doing a thing—he would always say straightforwardly exactly what he meant.

Even at Morris's speed of work the *Earthly Paradise*, being a large undertaking, continued to be written in and out of his daily life, as it were. The places that pleased him slipped into the monthly preludes to the tales. That for October recalls an autumn time at Southwold in 1868 in its first two lovely verses:

O Love, turn from the unchanging sea, and gaze
Down those grey slopes upon the year grown old,
A-dying mid the autumn-scented haze
That hangeth o'er the hollow in the wold,
Where the wind-bitten ancient elms enfold
Grey church, long barn, orchard, and red-roofed stead,
Wrought in dead days for men a long while dead.

Come down, O Love, may not our hands still meet,
Since still we live to-day, forgetting June,
Forgetting May, dreaming, October sweet—
—O hearken, hearken! through the afternoon,
The grey tower sings a strange old tinkling tune!
Sweet, sweet and sad, the toiling of year's last breath,
Too satiate of life to strive with death.

The inscription at the forefront of the *Earthly Paradise* was:

To my Wife

I Dedicate this Book

It had been the dream of both Morris and Burne-Jones that the one should illustrate the work of the other. Five hundred wood engravings were planned, and though a certain number of drawings were done and Morris himself tried his hand at engraving them before his illuminated crystal globe at Queen Square, the difficulties and the expense proved too great, and the idea had to be given up for the more straightforward publishing of F. S. Ellis. The writing of it and the publishing of it went on simultaneously. Even the necessity of taking his wife, who was in poor health, to Bad-Ems, did not deter Morris from his writing. Rossetti made a caricature of them at this time, showing Morris reading aloud to his wife, and called it "The Ms at Ems".

Of Bad-Ems Morris said he would consider it bearable if it did Janey any good, while as for himself, he was in "roaring and offensive health". He said he had not had any good wine while he was there, and evidently the mutton was tough, as he asks his correspondent: "Did you ever speculate as to what they fed German sheep on? Deep thought at breakfast time has led me to suppose indiarubber to be their pabulum."

5

The long task of writing and completing the *Earthly Paradise* was ended by the close of 1870, and as was but natural after so close and constant a kinship with many of the world's great stories, Morris found himself a little forlorn.

"I feel rather lost, at having done my book", he wrote: " I find now I liked working at it better than I thought. I must try to get something serious to do as soon as may be." There was a gap in his life. "One doesn't know sometimes how much service a thing has done us till it is gone."

Whether he realized it or not—and the probabilities are that he did not, for he was neither vain nor introspective— he had completed one of the great achievements of his life. When it was done he did not linger over it to sup up praise and consider that he—"the idle singer of an empty day", as he strangely called himself—had earned a space of leisure. Indeed, even before the *Earthly Paradise* was finished he had gone questing off on new adventures. The *Earthly Paradise* itself shows this in the Icelandic tales that crept in among the classical and romantic ones. He had made the discovery of that ancient region of the North which was to affect him so deeply and so strangely, and it was at once obvious to him that he must learn to speak and think in its language. Few men are eager, unless professed linguists, to learn a new tongue when they are in the latter half of their thirties. But Morris began his Icelandic studies in the year 1868, while he was still immersed in writing the *Earthly Paradise*. He learned Icelandic with Eirikr Magnússon and read with him the great Icelandic Sagas.

That was not enough for Morris: always thoroughgoing, the impression they had made upon him must take visible shape; he must translate them into English, so that others should share in that heroic heritage. He began to learn Icelandic in the autumn of 1868, and in the beginning of the next year the *Fortnightly Review* published his and Magnússon's joint translation of the "Saga of Gunnlang Worm-Tongue". This was to lead in due course to the translation of the "Grettis Saga" and the "Volsunga Saga", in collaboration with Magnússon—all of this being the solid foundations for the fabric of his own creation, *Sigurd the Volsung*, which was to appear later on. At this time he had not yet set foot in the country of the Sagas that had seized upon his mind and struck down to the iron of his inner core.

It was about this time that Watts painted his famous portrait of Morris, which has so much the look of a man who does not quite know where he is going, but feels it is to a far country.

6

In the year 1867 the Burne-Jones family left the house in Kensington where they had been living, and went to The Grange, North End Lane, Fulham—as that region was called in those days. The house had once been inhabited by Richardson, author of *Clarissa* and *Sir Charles Grandison*, and was dignified and charming. It was almost a country retreat, tall elm-trees stood rurally in the road; there were orchards and market-gardens round about, while The Grange itself had an ample garden. This was at the back of the house; a lawn, a little orchard where pear- and apple-trees bore fruit, a mound known as Pillicock Hill, and a fine old mulberry-tree.

At The Grange Burne-Jones was to live for the rest of his life—with the exception of the time he spent at Rotting-dean, in which Sussex seaside village he bought himself an abode facing the Green, which he named North End House after his home at Fulham—and at The Grange he died. Burne-Jones was quite definitely not a countryman; he observed the beauty of the visible world with a painter's eye, and his studio was his home.

This was not the case with Morris. His desire for a home of his own in the English country had gone unsatisfied ever since he had been obliged to abandon the Red House. "How jolly it would be to be in a little cottage in the deep country", he once said, "in the autumn country, which, after all, I love as much as the spring." He did not feel that a house in London was a home, particularly when he had two small daughters and a delicate wife. He had not even such a shadow of a country home as Burne-Jones was possessed of in The Grange at Fulham.

But a deep-felt and long-held desire usually brings its own fulfilment, and a great gift was coming to William Morris, something which was to make an essential part of

KELMSCOTT MANOR FROM THE SOUTH-EAST.

his life. He was the type of man to whom a house was a visible entity, something that had a life of its own, especially if it was an old house. Every feeling he possessed about a house, and every need of his personal life, was satisfied when he discovered Kelmscott Manor on the Upper Thames.

It seemed something more than mere chance when in the early spring of 1871 he saw the place advertised and went to look at it. "Kelmscott, a little village about two miles above Radcott Bridge," he wrote to Faulkner after he had seen it, "a heaven on earth; an old stone Elizabethan house like Water Eaton, and such a garden! Close down on the river and all things handy."

Kelmscott Manor is one of those small plain, perfect stone houses which enrich the Cotswold country and round about—a style of architecture in which simplicity and dignity are mingled in the rarest manner. After he had been living there for a score of years Morris wrote a description of it and of Kelmscott for a Guild magazine:

> . . . you come face to face with a mass of grey walls and pearly grey roofs which makes the house, called by courtesy the Manor House, though it seems to have no manorial rights attached to it, which I have held for twenty-three years. It lies at the very end of the village on a road which, brought up shortly by a backwater of the Thames, becomes a mere cart-track leading into the meadows along the river.
>
> Through a door in the high unpointed stone wall you go up a flagged path through the front garden to the porch. The house from this side is a lowish three-storied one with mullioned windows, and at right angles to this another block whose bigger windows and pedimented gable-lights indicate a later date. The house is built of well-laid rubble stone of the district, the wall of the latter part being buttered over, so to say, with thin plaster which has now weathered to the same colour as the stone of the walls; the roofs are covered with the beautiful stone slates of the district, the most lovely covering of which a roof can have, especially when, as here and in all the traditional old houses of the countryside, they are sized down; the smaller

4

ones to the top and the bigger ones towards the eaves, which gives one the same sort of pleasure in their orderly beauty as a fish's scales or a bird's feathers. . . .

Going under an arched opening in the yew hedge which makes a little garth about a low door in the middle of the north wall, one comes into a curious passage or lobby, a part of which is screened into a kind of pantry by wooden mullions which have once been glazed. The said lobby leads into what was once the great parlour (the house is not great at all, remember) and is now panelled with pleasing George I panelling, painted white: the chimney-piece is no doubt of the date of the building, and is of rude but rather amusing country work; the windows in this room are large and transomed, and it is as pleasant as possible; and I have many a memory of hot summer mornings passed in its coolness amidst the green reflections of its garden.

The tapestry room is over the big panelled parlour. The walls of it are hung with tapestry of about 1600, representing the story of Samson; they were never great works of art, and now when all the bright colours are faded out, and nothing is left but the indigo blues, the greys and the warm yellowy browns, they look better, I think, than they were meant to look: at any rate they make the walls a very pleasant background for the living people who haunt the room; and, in spite of the designer, they give an air of romance to the room which nothing else would quite do.

Another charm this room has, that through its south window you not only catch a glimpse of the Thames clover meadows and the pretty little elm-crowned hill over in Berkshire, but if you sit in the proper place, you can see not only the barn afore-said with its beautiful sharp gable, the grey stone sheds, and the dove-cote, but also the flank of the earlier house and its little gables and grey scaled roofs, and this is a beautiful out-look indeed.

A house that I love; with a reasonable love I think: for though my words may give you no idea of any special charm about it, yet I assure you that the charm is there; so much has the old house grown up out of the soil, and the lives of those that lived on it: some thin thread of tradition, a half-anxious sense of the delight of meadow and acre and wood and river; a certain amount (not too much, let us hope) of common sense, a liking for making materials serve one's turn, and perhaps at bottom some little grain of sentiment: this, I think, was what went to the making of the old house.

7

Such was Morris's straightforward yet tender description of his home when he had lived in it many years. There is a more impassioned and more famous one he wrote which will be quoted in due course, where he lets his heart speak with a note of pain under the thin veil of fiction.

As soon as he had discovered Kelmscott Manor, empty and waiting for him, he took his wife and Rossetti to look at it. The idea was that Rossetti should share the house with the Morris family—the rent was £60 a year—and this he did for a number of years, though Morris grew to like the arrangement less and less as time went on. He had grown completely away from Rossetti's influence in his maturity.

Morris's love for Kelmscott Manor so increased as the years went by that he wanted it without the alien and difficult presence of Dante Gabriel. But one permanent thing came from his presence at Kelmscott in the early days, and that was the many paintings he made of Jane Morris, then in the perfection of her melancholy beauty. He painted her under many titles, as Pandora, Silence, the Roseleaf, Aurea Catina, La Donna della Fiamma, and Proserpine. Prophetically, almost, his sister Christina wrote of his paintings:

> One face looks out from all his canvases,
> One selfsame figure sits or walks or leans:
> We found her hidden just behind those screens,
> That mirror gave back all her loveliness.
>
> A Queen in opal or in ruby dress,
> A nameless girl in freshest summer greens,
> A saint, an angel—every canvas means
> That one same meaning, neither more nor less.

There were, of course, two other women, Elizabeth Siddall and Fanny Schott, whom he painted with almost equal insistence, but it is actually Jane Morris who has come down to posterity as the Rossetti type. One of his loveliest paintings of her is called The Water Willow, where that dark sad face gazes at the beholder through willow boughs. Behind her head Kelmscott Manor is seen with its sharp gables against the sky, the wall with its narrow gate, and the river. It is a painting full of rich melancholy beauty, but very much "Marianna in the Moated Grange", and one feels it would be quite cheering to hear Topsy cursing when he was bitten by gnats as he fished by the river bank—a subject on which William De Morgan wrote a ribald little poem.

The fishing and boating at Kelmscott were of course very much part of its delights to Morris—he was by nature a waterman, and if the boat leaked and the boat-house was somewhat tumbledown, that would not disturb him. For practical comfort, as has been seen, he cared little; for visible beauty a great deal. On his first visit to Kelmscott Manor many years later when he had come into close contact and friendship with Morris, Sydney Cockerell said of Kelmscott:

> Except Hever and Ightham I don't think I have ever seen any house so beautiful. It looks as if it had risen from the ground with the old fruit trees about it, its grey stones, like them, tinted yellow with lichen.

In the early days of Kelmscott there was an old couple called Comely who kept an eye on the Manor House when the Morris family were absent. They had a cottage at the gates with a good garden for a rent of a shilling a week, and were, said a visitor, "the ideal English villagers, capable, careful, frugal, and industrious". The only thing that troubled Morris about old Comely was the automatic and feudal manner in which his hand rose to his forehead at every word he uttered when talking to his "betters". Morris, who certainly thought himself as good as any man, was also inclined to think, even before he was a diehard socialist, that any man was as good as himself —unless he was proved incompetent. But incompetence is not a word that can be associated with the old-fashioned English villager like Comely.

The joint tenancy of Kelmscott Manor with Rossetti soon showed signs of breaking down—Rossetti had claimed as his own the Tapestry Room, with the view which Morris described so lovingly—and in 1874 it finally came to an end. Rossetti's place as co-tenant was taken for a time by Morris's publisher and friend, F. S. Ellis.

The letters Morris wrote in his first year at Kelmscott, describing minutely, with his kind of medieval illuminator's eye, the growth of things in garden and field, and his increasing interest in birds—which continued with him for the rest of his life—show how much he was rejoicing in his old home in the deep quiet country. He was still obliged to be a great deal in London, owing to his work, but from then on Kelmscott was always the place where his heart dwelt.

This is shown with great beauty in the famous passage from the penultimate chapter of *News from Nowhere*, when Ellen says to the teller of that tale:

"Take me on to the house."
The raised way led us into a little field bounded by a backwater of the river on one side; on the right hand we could see a cluster of small houses and barns, new and old, and before us a grey stone barn and a wall partly overgrown with ivy, over which a few grey gables showed. The village road ended in the shallow of the aforesaid backwater. We crossed the road, and again almost without my will my hand raised the latch of a door in the wall, and we stood presently on a stone path which led up to the old house . . . the garden between the wall and the house was redolent of the June flowers, and the roses were rolling over one another with that delicious super-abundance of small well-tended gardens which at first sight takes away all thought from the beholder save that of beauty. The blackbirds were singing their loudest, the doves were cooing on the

roof-ridge, the rooks in the high elm-trees beyond were garrulous among the young leaves, and the swifts wheeled whining about the gables. And the house itself was a fit guardian for all the beauty of this heart of summer.

Once again Ellen echoed my thoughts as she said: "Yes, friend, this is what I came out for to see, this many-gabled old house built by the simple country-folk of the long-past times." . . . She led me up close to the house, and laid her shapely sun-browned hand and arm on the lichened wall as if to embrace it, and cried out, "O me! O me! How I love the earth, and the seasons, and weather, and all things that deal with it, and all that grows out of it—as this has done!". . .

She led me on to the door, murmuring little above her breath as she did so, "The earth and the growth of it and the life of it! If I could but say or show how I love it!"

We went in, and found no soul in any room as we wandered from room to room, from the rose-covered porch to the strange and quaint garrets amongst the great timbers of the roof, where of old times, the tillers and herdsmen of the manor slept. . . .

How close to the reality of Kelmscott Manor is that loving picture.

When, many years later, an edition of *News from Nowhere* was printed at the Kelmscott Press it had an enchanting frontispiece drawn by C. M. Greve, showing the front of Kelmscott Manor, the flagged path up to the simple porch, bordered by rose bushes, the gabled roof above which the doves flutter and settle in the sky brightening to sunset. Under this drawing are the words:

This is the Picture of the Old House by the Thames to which the People of this story went. Hereafter follows the Book itself which is called News from Nowhere or an Epoch of Rest and is written by William Morris.

Text and picture are both enclosed in a flowing leafy border designed by Morris. The whole thing is beautiful and satisfying, and shows how much "colour" there can be in black and white rightly handled.

8

The house at Kelmscott was to Morris like a house he had lived in during some previous stage of existence—he knew and loved it at once the moment his eyes fell on that grey gabled roof and he went through the door in the grey wall.

For twenty-five years he had the happiness of living there, and though he did not actually die under its roof, but at the house he had named after it on the banks of the same Thames at Hammersmith, as was right and proper, he was buried at Kelmscott. That little quiet village has gained a special kind of immortality because of him, its name is linked for ever with that of William Morris, and the Manor House he loved so much is now in the perpetual care of the University of Oxford. Its grey stone structure, the vast timbers upholding its lichened roof, its mullioned stone casements, its "dog-leg" staircase up and down which Morris went so eagerly, its tapestried room which he loved, from the window-seat of which he gazed at his favourite view, the solid oak Tudor chair where he sat at meals, and much of the decoration and furniture that was there in Morris's day, remains now in that safe keeping.

Morris himself never actually owned Kelmscott Manor —he had a lease of it from an old yeoman family named Hobbs. After his death Jane Morris bought it, and the property remained in the Morris family till the death of his daughter May in 1898, when it passed into the possession of the University of Oxford.

The village has another link with him in the cottages that Mrs. Morris had built in the local style of architecture as a memorial to her husband. One of these cottages bears a very simple almost childish carving, showing Morris sitting on the grass listening to the "small birdis" singing in the trees, at his side the leather satchel in which he used to carry the work upon which he was engaged—a poem or a pattern. It is all so homely and friendly that the cottage is usually referred to in the village as "the house where Mr. Morris is".

Morris, so deep a believer in the continuity of tradition, would like that. He is still there—if the villagers who knew him are gone, or going, their children still regard him as a person, not an abstraction. It all links up naturally with the pleasure he himself felt when he discovered at Great Coxwell Church, no great distance from Kelmscott, two brasses of the fifteenth century to William Morys "sutyme fermer of Cokyswell", and to Johane Morys his wife. He would almost think he and Jane were these two come alive again after three centuries or so, and living not far from their old home.

It was of Kelmscott Manor and of such memories that Morris said:

> It has come to be to me the type of the pleasant places of the earth, and of the homes of harmless, simple people not over-burdened with the intricacies of life; and as others love the race of man through their lovers or their children, so I love the earth through that small space of it.

For the noble barn at Great Coxwell, Morris had a passionate admiration, and called it one of the noblest buildings in England, if not in the world. All the visitors at Kelmscott Manor had to be taken to see it, and Morris wrote of it on one occasion:

> The harvest being now out of the barn we saw the corbels that support the wall-pieces: they are certainly not later than 1250: so the barn is much earlier than I thought: the building of the walls and buttresses is remarkably good and solid.

A friend of his said that Morris loved Great Coxwell barn "not only deeply but excitedly".

9

The year 1871 was a notable one in Morris's life. He was thirty-eight years old. He had completed his long task of writing the *Earthly Paradise*. He had taken the lease of Kelmscott Manor at midsummer, and in July he went down there with Janey and the children, to help them to settle in their new enchanting home.

Then leaving them and the house which had so taken and was to hold his heart for the rest of his life, he set off on a journey to Iceland—so remote from mellow Kelmscott and all it stood for. One of his friends said of Morris that he had the unaccountable restlessness of a wild animal. He had an infinite patience in the use of his hands when engaged on any craft work, combined with an infinite impatience or restlessness of his mind—always questing, always pursuing. That "hooded look" about his eyes, their outer inexpressiveness, was partly protective—aware of his own apparently unaccountable urge to action he kept a certain guard. A bird's swift movements seem erratic to the beholder, but the bird has his own chart, knows where he is going.

Morris had been hearing the call of Iceland for some time. The summer of moving into a new house might not seem the best time to answer it, but trifling considerations of convenience or what was suitable never disturbed Topsy in the least.

The importance of this first journey to Iceland, says Morris's biographer, J. W. Mackail, can hardly be over-estimated, and "even to those who knew him well, was not wholly intelligible. To enter into his feelings one must imagine a strange combination of Johnson in the Hebrides and Byron in Greece."

But in reality Morris on the verge of forty was much younger than Dr. Johnson and Byron had ever been in their lives.

4*

The journey to Iceland was no doubt undertaken in response to some inner need which the study of Icelandic literature had revealed in him—like the drink of iced water after a glut of sweetmeats. It answered some fundamental boyishness and roughness in him which was overlaid by his decorative life and his artistic friends, but which was there all the time. His delicate childhood, his serious youth, his close friendship with Burne-Jones, had hidden it. Burne-Jones had no concealed longings to be a pirate, a Viking, or that captain of the "Swallow". But Topsy had, and as he grew to maturity these longings came out in his rough and careless attire, his extraordinary capacity for getting himself dirty, just as small boys do, his passion for fishing and boats, his passion for Iceland—and later on in his untidy socialism, which so disturbed all his friends. He cared nothing for what was respectable, and he lived in a very respectable era. It was as though one part of him was bursting through its civilized trappings into a kind of reality without which it could not breathe fully. Nearly all his friends admired his every action and achievement and idea, save his ideas on socialism—and this lack of support in something he vitally needed no doubt helped to drive him into himself, made him more shut up and secret and indifferent to human contacts than he would have been.

Anyway, the first journey to Iceland was a glorious break away from civilized life and a return to the primitive. In 1871 it really was going into the wilds—it meant providing all one's own equipment, it meant camping out with ponies, tents, food, and finding the way across rough, uncouth, threatening country.

Morris had three companions in this adventure—his teacher of Icelandic, Eirikr Magnússon, his old friend Charles Faulkner, and a new friend, W. H. Evans of Forde Abbey in Dorset, who was interested in Iceland.

Once they left Reykjavik the little party would be out of touch with the world, and one of the pleasures of the trip that Topsy anticipated keenly was doing his own cooking, for which he had a considerable gift. How like a school-boy he was in view of this expedition is shown by the way in which he came one day into the Burne-Jones' garden at The Grange, and built a little out-of-doors fireplace of loose bricks on which he cooked a savoury stew. He was practising for the wilds of Iceland.

Until this journey to Iceland, Morris had never even been as far north as Scotland, and when he saw the Faeroe Islands he confessed that he shuddered at his first sight of a "really northern land in the grey of a coldish morning". But on his return journey the Faeroes seemed to him "such a gentle sweet place when we saw them again after Iceland".

Morris, who declared he was no good at writing letters, had decided to keep a diary of all that he saw in Iceland, and he did so very fully and faithfully, describing things with great vividness and detail, as if he were weaving a tapestry background for the great figures of the Icelandic Sagas. There was some idea that this diary might be published, but Morris decided against doing so, and it was not till after his death that it was published complete in the eighth volume of his *Collected Works*, though portions of it were used by Mackail in his biography.

Of his first sight of Iceland Morris wrote to his wife:

It is no use trying to describe it, but it was quite up to my utmost expectations as to strangeness: it is just like nothing else in the world; it was a wild morning too, very black out to sea, and very bright sun under a sort of black canopy over Iceland.

And he wrote a poem about it too, "Iceland First Seen", of which the first three verses out of six are these:

Lo from our loitering ship a new land at last to be seen;
Toothed rocks down the side of the firth on the east guard a
    weary wide lea,
And black slope the hillsides above, striped adown with their
    desolate green:

And a peak rises up on the west from the meeting of cloud
  and of sea,
Foursquare from base unto point like the building of Gods
  that have been,
The last of that waste of the mountains all cloud-wreathed
  and snow-flecked and grey,
And bright with the dawn that began just now at the ending
  of day.

Ah! what came we forth for to see that our hearts are so hot
  with desire?
Is it enough for our rest, the sight of this desolate strand,
And the mountain-waste, voiceless as death but for winds
  that may sleep not nor tire?
Why do we long to wend forth, through the length and
  breadth of a land,
Dreadful with grinding of ice, and the record of scarce hidden
  fire,
But that there 'mid the grey grassy dales sore scarred by the
  ruining streams
Lives the tale of the Northland of old and the undying glory
  of dreams?

O land, as some cave by the sea where the treasures of old
  have been laid,
The sword it may be of a king whose name was the turning
  of fight:
Or the staff of some wise of the world that many things made
  and unmade,
Or the ring of a woman maybe whose woe is grown wealth
  and delight.
No wheat and no wine grows above it, no orchard for blossom
  and shade;
The few ships that sail by its blackness but deem it the mouth
  of a grave;
Yet sure when the world shall awaken, this too shall be
  mighty to save.

The sorrow, both in landscape and saga, of Iceland,
drew Morris very strangely. In his poem, "To the Muse

of the North"—which was written first as an introduction
to his translation of the *Grettis Saga*—he says:

> O Mother, and Love, and Sister all in one
> Come thou; for sure I am enough alone
> That thou thine arms about my heart shouldst throw,
> And wrap me in the grief of long ago.

It was this oddly mixed being, the poet, athirst for
ancient sorrows, for "old, unhappy, far-off things", and the
small boy eager for adventure, who first stepped on the
Icelandic shore in July 1871.

In the introduction to the volume containing Morris's
Icelandic Journals, his daughter May says of him with
tender understanding:

> He was entirely absorbed in the country they went through;
> it is curious to see how little mention is made of persons. One
> gets an impression that for the time he had shaken off his
> human sympathies, that people did not interest him—he had
> no need for them—and that he had withdrawn into a frame of
> mind in which he saw the wilderness in its real loneliness, awful,
> unlovable and remote from human life—the elemental horrors
> had seized upon him and perhaps he saw sights and heard
> sounds from another world than that in which he and his
> fellow-travellers were moving—who knows indeed where the
> poet wanders when he withdraws into his own country?

The route of the journey was planned for the purpose
of seeing the places connected with the great Sagas, places
which appealed to Morris far more than the extraordinary
Geysirs which to most tourists are the principal attraction
of Iceland. Morris was very indignant that the Geysirs
were all that ordinary people knew about Iceland—people
who "have never heard the names of Sigurd and Brynhild,
of Djal, or Gunnar, or Grettir, or Gisli or Gudrun".

He found the long days riding the sturdy indigenous
ponies very exhilarating, and enjoyed doing the camp
cooking—he was soon discovered to be by far the best
cook of the party—but did not like shooting for the pot,

and was annoyed with his gun which, he said, wanted as "much attention as a baby with croup". Of his first cooking efforts he says:

> I was patient, I was bold, and the results were surprising even to me who suspected my own hidden talents in the matter: a stew was this trial piece; a stew, four plovers or curlews, a piece of lean bacon and a tin of carrots.

A few extracts from Morris's first Icelandic Journal will give glimpses of his experiences. This journal is quite a lengthy and detailed document, written in an extremely simple and straightforward way, describing somewhat monotonous happenings in a somewhat monotonous manner, though impressive in a stark way about that stark country. There are no treasures of art and architecture to talk about—just daily journeyings on pony back, the small mishaps of camping, fording constant rivers, drinking coffee in a turf house with one or two of the sparse inhabitants. The remarkable thing is that out of these thin materials Morris has made a curiously fascinating narrative. One reads on with an eager interest for the next small event, and all the while in the background is forming a looming picture of the ancient Iceland Morris loved where life seemed on a much more heroic scale than it was in his day.

His first impression of the mainland was of :

> a terrible shore indeed: a great mass of dark grey mountains worked into pyramids and shelves, looking as if they had been built and half ruined; they were striped with snow high up, and wreaths of cloud dragged across them here and there.

A little later he wrote:

> Most strange and awful the country looked to me as we passed through, in spite of all my anticipations: a doleful land at first with its great rubbish heaps of sand, striped scantily with green grass sometimes; varied though by a bank of sweet grass here and there full of flowers, and little willowy grey-leaved plants.

But in spite of the bleakness he found the "whole scene was impressive and exciting: as almost always was the case in Iceland, there was nothing mean or prosaic to jar upon one in spite of the grisly desolation."

This effect of desolation was greatly increased by the many white streams, mostly glacier streams, running between banks of black sand, with here and there patches of earth burnt red or orange by extinct crater fires.

The Morris party on their ponies often journeyed under great cliffs and crevasses that reduced them to midgets. The cliffs were often :

> unimaginably strange: they overhang in some places much more than seemed possible; they had caves in them just like the hell-mouths in thirteenth century illuminations; or great straight pillars were rent from them with quite flat tops of grass and a sheep or two feeding on it, however the devil they got there.

In spite of his passionate and historically based interest in Iceland, the country got him down now and again, and he felt a desperate longing for his home in the mellow old house at Kelmscott. Iceland, he says once when at Herdholt:

> is an awful place: set aside the hope that the unseen sea gives you here, and the strange threatening change of the blue spiky mountains beyond the firth, and the rest seems emptiness and nothing else: a piece of turf under your feet, and the sky overhead, that's all; whatever solace your life is to have must come out of yourself or these old stories, not over hopeful themselves.

Nevertheless he rejoiced to say:

> I have seen many marvels, and some terrible pieces of country; slept in the home-field of Djal's home and Gunnar's, and at Herdholt; I have seen Bjarg, and Bathstead, and the place where Bolli lived, and am now a half-hour's ride from where Gudrun died. I was there yesterday, and from its door you see a great sea of terrible inky mountains tossing about.

In Morris's mind all the while he travelled this desolate land, was the background of the great Sagas—he knew and saluted each cleft and hill where the Icelandic heroes had lived and died, slain and been slain. When he came to Thingvellir and the Hill of Laws, he wrote:

> Once again that thin thread of insight and imagination, which comes so seldom to us, and is such a joy when it comes, did not fail me at this first sight of the greatest marvel and most storied place in Iceland.

To Morris, in spite of his speaking of its coming so seldom, that "thin thread" was rarely absent—it linked all the labours of his life together.

The account he gives at the end of this journal of his return to civilization is very good and without flourishes. On the journey south from Edinburgh he thought that:

> the houses and horses looked so disproportionately big for the landscape that it all looked like a scene at a theatre.

"So there I was in London at last," he wrote,

> well washed, and finding nobody I cared for dead: a piece of luck that does not always happen to people when they are fools enough to go away beyond call for more than two months.

10

Two years later, almost to a day, Morris made a second journey to Iceland, and Charles Faulkner again went with him. He found in that country on the very edge of the world something that had a deep appeal to him, and after his several journeys there he said:

> The journey has deepened the impression I had of Iceland and increased my love for it. The glorious simplicity of the terrible and tragic, but beautiful land, with its well-remembered stories of brave men, killed all querulous feeling in me,

and has made all the dear faces of wife and children I love and friends dearer than ever to me. I feel as if a definite space of my life had passed away now I have seen Iceland for the last time: as I looked up at Charles' wain to-night, all my travel there seemed to come back on me, made solemn and elevated in one moment till my heart swelled with the wonder of it: surely I have gained a great deal, and it was no idle whim that drew me there, but a true instinct for what I needed.

As was only natural after his deeply felt experiences in Iceland, he found a certain smugness in the English scene —the comfortable houses with their "bedded out" gardens, their geraniums and calceolarias, their glass-houses and conventions. But happily Kelmscott was still perfect— "my own little home by Lechlade though, is sweet and innocent enough," he wrote, "and though it has a sadness about it, which is not shown, but the melancholy born of beauty, I suppose, it is very stimulating to the imagination."

A new inhabitant at Kelmscott was the sturdy native pony, christened Mouse, on whose back Morris had ridden over so much of Iceland—"the bravest and best-tempered of little beasts", he called it. The Morris children were enchanted with Mouse, and petted and fed him, and rode him about the countryside, and also drove him about the lanes in a little basket-carriage. Needless to say, under this treatment, after his much harder life in Iceland, Mouse grew fat and lazy, though it is recorded that on one occasion when the Hunt went by, the fat Iceland pony jumped the hedge of his paddock and set off on his own to follow the English hounds.

Mouse is about the only animal to come into Morris's life. He did not care for dogs, and his kind of life did not bring him much in contact with horses—though he said once that they were creatures of whom he could have grown fond.

Before his second visit to Iceland in the summer of 1873 Morris made his first visit to Italy in company with Burne-Jones. But something in his mind, so responsive to Gothic

France, refused Italy. Perhaps with Iceland before and behind him, he found Italian beauty too rich and too luxurious, and with a great deal of Italian art and architecture he was definitely out of tune. His answer to a friend who was urging Morris to accompany him to Rome, fantastic though it is, shows his temper: "Do you suppose that I shall see in Rome", he asked, "what I can't see in Whitechapel?"

One thing is quite certain—he could not see in Whitechapel the London "small and white and clean", which he imagined in the Prologue of the *Earthly Paradise*. But then he never could have seen that, even in the thirteenth century.

However, the fact remains—to be recorded and then put aside—that Italy was not one of the moulders of Morris's mind. He was English and he was Gothic, with a sudden stark volcanic rock which was Iceland, starting up amid the meadows and the cathedrals. Morris had the great strength—indeed it is one of the smaller signs of genius—never to touch anything that did not belong to him. He knew his own things by instinct and seized them with a fierce possessiveness. The other things, however praised by mankind, however much considered necessary and desirable, he simply ignored.

Two other qualities he had—apparently contradictory qualities—an urgent sense of the importance of Time:

> But at my back I always hear
> Time's winged chariot hurrying near,

combined with a rare capacity for idleness. So many of his friends testify that however busy he was—and he was always busy—he could also invariably find time to go on boating expeditions, to go fishing, to play bowls. To do anything, in fact, that he thought nice. Yet the actual amount of work he got through, visual work that exists in concrete shape, quite apart from his business and the causes to which he gave his time, show how continuously and fruitfully occupied he always was.

II

It is not necessary to say much about Morris's second Iceland visit. He spent two months there and deepened his first impressions, gathering the impulse and the feeling which were to go to the making of his great epic *Sigurd the Volsung*, which in its scale and its strange apprehension of the Icelandic past, might have been sung by one of the ancient skalds who belonged there by birth and inheritance.

Few of Morris's friends shared this Northern enthusiasm of his. Burne-Jones declared that he hoped he'd never go farther north than Hampstead, and when Morris returned from his second Iceland journey he wrote to a friend saying that Topsy had "come back more enslaved with passion for ice and snow and raw fish than ever—I fear I shall never drag him to Italy again". He made a little sketch of a fur-clad Topsy squatting among icebergs savagely gnawing at a huge raw fish.

After his first contact with the remote North the Icelandic part of Morris retreated into a volcanic cave, as it were, and lay brooding and absorbing experience in quiet. It was some years before he completed *Sigurd the Volsung*.

As can easily be imagined, Morris's view of the great Northern Sagas was extremely different from those of Richard Wagner, and when someone sent him a translation of the libretto of *Die Walkure* he wrote back in some anger:

> I look upon it as nothing short of desecration to bring such a tremendous and world-wide subject under the gaslights of an opera: the most rococo and degraded of all forms of art—the idea of a sandy-haired German tenor tweedledeeing over the unspeakable woes of Sigurd, which even the simplest words are not typical enough to express! Excuse my heat: but I wish to see Wagner uprooted.

But even to Morris there were other things than Iceland.

He became absorbed in the delicate art of illuminating; he wrote one of the gentlest of his poems in *Love is Enough*.

In his designing of pattern the bold and the delicate were equally within his scope; he was not a man of one manner, as is seen by comparing the great bold acanthus sweeps of some of his foliage designs, and the faery delicacy of his illuminating work. "So fair a land, so small a land", Morris said in one of his early stories, for he had the medieval craftsman's love for smallness, for things within the natural scope and grasp of the hands, for the illuminated vignette in a Book of Hours, for the close carving of a bench-end or a chest. The modern passion for judging things by their size, the bigger the finer, had not touched him, and never did. He had the patience for fine work, in spite of his general tempestuousness, and his big hands were endowed with the necessary delicacy. His daughter, in one of her introductions to his *Collected Works*, has a charming account of watching him at work, his fine big head bent over his minute toil, his precision and delicacy in the use of the fragile gold leaf, the way in which he would paint flowers that almost needed a microscope to behold. Work so fine that the craftsman had to hold his breath as he did it was exquisite and enjoyable to Topsy, little as it seemed in character at times. But he had an infinite patience with the materials he could shape to lasting beauty. A friend one day found him filling in the background of a design with spots, and asked why ever he did not get someone else to do that part of it for him. "Do you think", asked an astonished Morris, "that I am such a fool, after having had the grind of doing the design, as to let another man have the fun of putting in the dots?"

The first long poem Morris wrote after his visit to Iceland was as remote as might be from that bleak country; it was a return to the romantic dream of his youth, softened and more tender. This poem was *Love is Enough*, and Burne-Jones said of it:

He makes a poem these days—in dismal Queen Square in black old filthy London in dull end of October he makes a pretty poem that is to be wondrously happy; and it has four sets of lovers in it and *they are all happy* and it ends well, and will come out some time next summer, and I shall make little ornaments to it—such is Top in these days.

A somewhat more comprehensive idea of Morris as a poet is given by this extract from an admirable notice in the *Daily Chronicle* written after his death:

In the poetry of Morris all his passion for imperfect Utopias past, and perfect Utopias to come, all his hatred of monstrous modernity, all his sense of life as a thing capable of being and meant to be radiant, joyous, unoppressed, found their true form. The *Defence of Guenevere*, the *Life and Death of Jason*, the *Earthly Paradise*, the *Story of Sigurd, Love is Enough, Poems by the Way*, with translations of the *Odyssey* and *Aeneid*—what worship of beauty is in these! Beauty in a very wide and full sense, including beauty of battle and storm, of action and passion, not less than of things peaceful and at rest, things comely and calm. Beginning with a mystical and remote world of enchantment, he became gradually more and more enamoured of a fresh and simple world, romantic indeed, but conceivable; and he ended with songs for socialists, practical march music for the Israelites *in exitu de Aegypto*. From a personal passion for beauty, he came to hunger for its universal empire among men, beauty of work and of pleasure, beauty for the common weal.

The masque of *Love is Enough* gives glimpses of a mystical side of Morris which he very rarely revealed. Perhaps because of this in later years he did not much like the poem. In his admirable book, *The Kelmscott Press and William Morris, Master-Craftsman*, Halliday Sparling has this revealing little story. On one occasion Morris and some of his friends were talking very seriously when Morris "electrified those present by snatching down the volume [*Love is Enough*] from his bookshelves, rapping upon it with a paper-knife, pointing to its title, and exclaiming: 'There's a lie for you, though 'twas I that told it! Love isn't

enough in itself; love *and work*, yes! *Work* and love, that's
the life of a man! Why, a fellow can't even love decently
unless he's got work to do, and pulls his weight in the
boat!'"

12

For a year before he went to Iceland Morris had been,
with all his usual zest in acquiring a new craft, studying
the art of illuminating, and on his return from his first
journey, resumed it eagerly. He not only illuminated
several books—one of them a collection of his own verses,
which he gave to Georgiana Burne-Jones, and another *The
Rubá'iyát* of Omar Khayyám—but wrote them out by hand
as well in a beautiful calligraphy. J. W. Mackail has a
very interesting passage on this matter:

> Morris's own handwriting had been then, and for years
> afterwards continued to be, decidedly bad: while not illegible,
> it was slovenly, and had neither beauty nor distinction. When
> he took up the art of illumination in 1870, he began to study
> handwriting as a fine art. By practice he soon mastered it, and
> the texts of his painted books show a steady advance in skill of
> execution. The reaction on his own cursive hand was marked
> and immediate. The beautiful handwriting familiar to his
> friends for the last five and twenty years was directly due to his
> study and practice of the art in the periods of his work as an
> illuminator. In the decoration of his painted books—as in
> everything which had to do with pattern and colour—there
> is also an advance in splendour of colouring and breadth of
> design, but the earliest are in their simpler treatment as faultless
> as the latest: the art of decoration seems to have been born in
> him and to come from his hands full-grown.

After he had acquired his beautiful scribe's hand even
his ordinary copy for the printer became a joy to behold,
though the result of that, as he complained, was: "I am

worse printed than any other author, and that is because my 'copy' is so clear that the compositors hand it over to the apprentices to set up."

13

During the middle period of his life Morris was to make two more moves. Kelmscott Manor remained till his death the house of his heart, but it was his country retreat. By the necessities of his work he was obliged to have also a house in London; he could not rush from that old grey house by the "baby Thames" every time his presence was needed at the dyeworks or the printing-press.

The London home the Morris family had made, considerably against the grain, had to be given up entirely to the increasing needs of the business, so Morris had to find somewhere else for his wife and children to live at such times as they were not enjoying the summer and autumn beauties of Kelmscott. For himself, apart from the claims of the firm and its workshops, it was needful that he should not be cut off from contact with his friends and clients in London. Therefore it became necessary that somewhere in or near London he must have a house. It was probably the fact of Burne-Jones being settled in Fulham—West Kensington as it is now called—which directed his attention to the not very attractive westerly suburbs of Turnham Green and Hammersmith. Another thing that perhaps made him look that way, instead of towards the more favoured Hampstead or Highgate, was probably the proximity of the Thames. He liked water and boats and fishing.

So at Turnham Green he found a residence called Horrington House, now regrettably pulled down, which, though small, was secluded and had a high wall round a good garden. It was next door to an inn, which was a house of call for the country wagons of produce coming in to London, so that as his daughter said, "one got a breath of country life in the loads of market stuff and the leisurely carters with their long whips".

Also down Chiswick Lane, Horrington House was within easy reach of the river. It is a pleasant thought to imagine the burly William Morris, with his seafaring appearance, walking down Chiswick Lane—perhaps stopping at the ancient timbered inn for a glass of beer—and strolling up and down in the sunshine on Chiswick Mall, with the Thames on one side of him and on the other the enchanting and unspoiled old houses—Strawberry House, Walpole House, Bedford House, and the others, which make up that little oasis of the grace and distinction of a past day.

At Horrington House Morris lived for six years. He had left Queen Square without any tearing up of roots. He only really gave his heart twice to a house, first to Red House which he had built and adorned with so much youthful joy, and finally to Kelmscott Manor. His other abodes, though he beautified and adorned them as he could not help doing, were just places in which it was convenient and necessary to live.

When at the end of that six years he moved to his last London home it was to Kelmscott House on the Upper Mall at Hammersmith, facing direct on to the Thames, with only a narrow roadway between the house and the river. It was not called Kelmscott House when he went there, but by the somewhat gloomy name—which Morris said reminded him of a home for the insane—of The Retreat. There was one hundred and thirty miles of river between the house at Kelmscott and the house at Hammersmith, and it pleased Morris to connect his two homes not only by water but by name—the water that had passed one, in due course swirled, deepened and dirtied, past the other.

The immediate previous tenant of The Retreat had been George Macdonald, the author of *At the Back of the North Wind* and the *Curdie* stories. But however good his books, his taste in house decoration was not Morris's. The

KELMSCOTT HOUSE, HAMMERSMITH.

living-room walls were covered with a red flock paper, with long bookcases painted black, the ceilings azure blue, spotted with tarnished gilt stars. But Morris had no difficulty in altering all that; his business was in the full flood of its activities and production, and he could lay his hand straightaway on the wallpapers, hangings, curtains, rugs, shapes, and colours he required.

Kelmscott House itself is a plain simple late Georgian residence, with a garden of a rural spaciousness at the back. It was built in the period when Hammersmith was still a village, even if not quite so early as the time Bowack spoke of in 1705, when Hammersmith, in his words, "has several good houses in and about it, inhabited by gentry and persons of quality, and for above a hundred years past, has been a summer retreat for nobility and wealthy citizens, especially from about the year 1620 and the late unnatural rebellion".

If in Morris's day Gaggle-Goose Green had disappeared, Hampshire Hog Lane was still in existence, and there remained faint suggestions of a rural past still to be found in Hammersmith.

Morris wrote to his wife describing Kelmscott House:

> The situation is certainly the prettiest in London . . . the house could easily be done up at a cost of money: the long drawing-room, with a touch of my art, could be made one of the prettiest in London: the garden is really most beautiful. If you come to think of it, you will find that you won't get a garden or a house with much character unless you go out about as far as the Upper Mall. I don't think that either you or I could stand a quite modern house in a street. I don't fancy going back among the bugs of Bloomsbury.

The Morris family moved in to Kelmscott House in the autumn of 1878, and some of their earliest treasures came to adorn the latest home. The long drawing-room on the first floor, with its five windows looking through the tall elm-trees on to the sparkling or the sullen river, was hung with the Morris Blue Bird chintz. The famous painted

settle and cabinet from Red House were also there. The
carpet was blue, with lovely Eastern rugs on it. And on
the ceiling was the wavering, watery light of the river,
which is one of the adornments of a riverside house, lighting
up the rich colours of fabrics and carpets. It was a beautiful
room, and all who knew it were enchanted with it. But
though he saw at once the possibilities and charms of that
long first-floor room, Morris had nothing good to say about
the very fine dining-room on the garden side of the house,
with its big curved window. It was eighteenth-century
Adam in style, and Morris did not like the totally un-Gothic
Adam, and in his extravagant way declared the noble room
was only fit to keep pigs and hens in, or let out as a dis-
senters' chapel. But when it had been painted white and
hung with Morris's charming Pimpernel wallpaper, with a
white dresser laden with blue china, with a gorgeous
Persian carpet hung on one wall and one of Rossetti's
paintings of Jane Morris over the fireplace, it was a very
beautiful room, though not the kind of room that Morris
cared for most, though he had removed it as far as possible
from Adam by his decorative treatment.

Morris himself, in his study which was at the front of the
house looking to the Thames, was content with bare oak
shelves and a bare oak table, without any hangings or
adornments at all. In his bedroom, to which a little stair
led from the book-lined study, he had a loom set up so
that he could work at his new joy of tapestry-weaving at
any hour when the impulse took him. He was an early
riser.

Kelmscott House had a really large and secluded garden,
with tall trees, including a fine tulip-tree on the lawn, an
orchard, and fruit trees on the old walls at the back of the
house. There were also ample coach-houses and stabling,
for which Morris soon found many uses. A door in the
garden wall opened into Hampshire Hog Lane, a name
which pleasantly recalled to Morris the Hog's Hole close
to Red House at Upton.

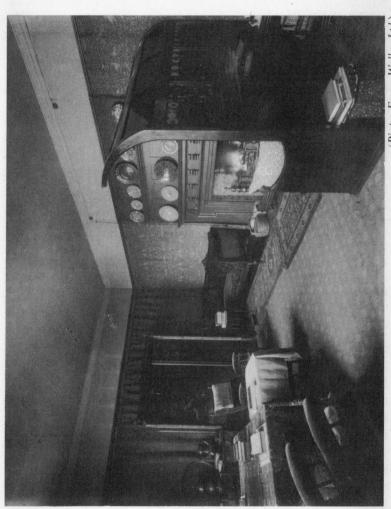

KELMSCOTT HOUSE: THE DINING ROOM.

Kelmscott House soon became a pleasant abode to Morris and his wife and daughters.

"It was", says May Morris,

> scarcely London, with the great elms along the river-front and the sun-reflections dancing on the wide water. We felt the changes of the seasons there, all the happenings of the weather, as no Londoner can do . . . when a gale came we could see the squall hurrying from the west, and Thames beaten into waves and foam.

"There is something touching", wrote Morris one autumn, "about the real world bursting into London with these gales."

14

William Morris's two daughters were growing out of their childhood, though for long enough he affectionately called them "the littles". As was natural with such parents, they were both beautiful girls, in the Rossetti–Burne-Jones manner, accentuated by their way of wearing their hair and their artistic and unfashionable clothing. The fashions of the period were particularly ugly, and it was not to be expected that any of Morris's womenkind would wear them. In one of his lectures Morris said with considerable daring:

> There are two things about which women know absolutely nothing, dress and cookery; their twist isn't that way. They have no sense of colour or grace in drapery, and they never invented a new dish or failed to half spoil an old one.

In the year 1871 Rossetti drew portrait heads of both Jenny the elder and May the younger daughter. Of these two, May is the most Burne-Jones-like, with her large eyes, rather long nose, beautiful mouth and jawbone, and graceful mop of hair. Jenny has the same full and well-cut mouth, in both cases inherited from their mother, but in other ways, through her girlish charm, has a definite touch of her father, and a thoughtful look. Morris himself was intensely proud of his daughters.

"They are such big girls", he wrote in 1875, "and so good; and even handsome. Me! What a boy I feel still to have that responsibility on me."

A year earlier the Morris and Burne-Jones families were photographed in a group together at Fulham, against the garden wall of The Grange. It is an extremely interesting and faintly funny picture. Mrs. Morris and Mrs. Burne-Jones are sitting together on a bench, Mrs. Morris with Jenny by her side, and Mrs. Burne-Jones with her little son Philip. Behind their respective wives are the two husbands, with their daughters, May, and the small Margaret Burne-Jones, who was to marry Morris's biographer, J. W. Mackail. Though all grouped together in this way, the Morris family look considerably bigger than the Burne-Jones family, who seem to have shrunk. Georgiana Burne-Jones appears no larger than her young son, and with her conventional dark dress, her plainly banded smooth hair, is eclipsed in every sense by the beautiful Janey, who looms above her in light-coloured flowing robes, with her rich and decorative hair, looking lovely, though rather gloomy. So far as can be recalled there is no photograph or picture of her looking gay and smiling. The two Morris girls are dressed in long-skirted and rather shapeless and bulky gowns, no doubt beautiful as to colour and texture, with heavy beads round their necks. Behind his wife Topsy stands with his crest of hair, looking stout and vigorous, his right hand with a pipe in it, resting on the shoulder of his younger daughter. Shrinking as far as possible in the background, looking very like the thin bearded "Bogey" he was so fond of drawing as himself, is Burne-Jones.

These "group photographs", though often doing less than justice to the individuals in them, are generally revealing and full of interest. In this group of two such eminent and artistic families it is amusing to find the usual mixture of defiance, boredom, and shyness in the expressions of the different sitters.

In spite of Mrs. William Morris's remarkable beauty, because of her manner of dressing four centuries behind the mode, when the family went abroad the Gallic on-lookers were inclined to point and giggle at her. This roused her husband to such rage that he had sometimes to be forcibly restrained by his friends from violence.

When he went abroad in his later years, which he did now and then, it was more for the benefit of his wife's health and his daughters' happiness and education than for his own particular pleasure. But May Morris has told what an exciting person he was to travel with, and what a glow and vitality all things took on when he described and explained them. His own pleasure he found principally in his masculine journeys to Iceland, and in the gentle, faintly melancholy beauty of Kelmscott Manor.

15

Soon after Morris gave up the Queen Square house to his business, and lived first at Turnham Green and then at Hammersmith, the affairs of the firm came to breaking-point. On the surface it was very flourishing, but there was trouble underneath. This trouble concerned the part-ners, the original partners, who had each put a few pounds into the business at the beginning, and who had each been paid for any work they did. The financial needs of the young firm were more or less supplied first by Morris's mother and then by himself. It is unnecessary to go into all the details, which in this day are not specially interesting except for the way they reveal the characters of the men involved. Two things are plain: how sturdy was Morris's back for bearing any necessary burdens, and how little he cared about money as money. On the other hand, Rossetti in spite of his romantic pictures and poems, had it is evident a good deal of Shylock in his nature, and without either grace or gratitude demanded the return of his bond. Morris for a long time had been feeling Rossetti a trial, and over this matter their friendship came to a final end. Rossetti really wanted a tool and a satellite, and Morris was not meant by nature for either of those parts.

At the beginning of 1873 Morris wrote to an old friend about the firm and his own attitude towards it:

> I should very much like to make the business quite a success, and it can't be, unless I work at it myself. I must say, though I don't call myself money-greedy, a smash on that side would be a terrible nuisance; I have so many serious troubles, pleasures, hopes and fears, that I have not time on my hands to be ruined and get really poor: above all things it would destroy my freedom of work, which is a dear delight to me.

When the firm was started there were six partners, Rossetti being one. They put very little money in, and for years there was little to take out, though this was not the case in 1874, when the business was flourishing; but it was flourishing almost entirely because of the money, the skill, the inventiveness, the energy, that Morris had put into it. But this was not recognized by Rossetti, Marshall, and Madox Brown, who demanded their full legal share of the profits, to which they had contributed so little. Burne-Jones, Charles Faulkner, and Philip Webb refused to make this unjust and unreasonable claim, and finally after a period of strain, difficulty and distress to Morris, the firm was officially dissolved and began afresh under William Morris's sole name and ownership. This was in March 1875.

Queen Square was entirely given over to the business, except for one room Morris kept for himself, where he was looked after by a housekeeper who, he said, was "like a troll-wife in an Icelandic story, with a deep bass voice".

However, as he had a beautiful wife and two fair daughters at home, no doubt he was able to bear this.

Feeling that the firm of Morris & Company was now really in his own hands, he attacked all its problems with even increased energy. Dyeing was one of the great problems. In the early days Morris had to rely on the dyed materials he could purchase from the manufacturers, and it was only his own skill that made anything attractive out of the peacock-blues, the rust-reds, and the olive-greens which were then the best colours obtainable.

"I am most deeply impressed", Morris wrote, "with the importance of our having all our dyes the soundest and best that can be, and am prepared to give up all that part of my business which depends on textiles if I fail in getting them so."

As soon as he got his own dye vats he used the permanent dyestuffs, indigo blues, madder reds, weld yellows. He had no love for indeterminate bilious "art" shades. This shocked some of his would-be artistic customers, one of whom complained that the "Hammersmith" carpets were too bright to be really tasteful. "If you want mud," said Morris, who happened to be in the showroom, "you can find it in the road outside!"

Morris taught himself the whole art of dyeing. He declared he was "taking in dyeing at every pore", which was true enough, as for days on end his hands were such a sight that they even troubled his own robust and un-finicky nature. But that he should do it himself was the only way in which he could get the colours he wanted and be able to teach others. But there are certain fine shades of skill and craft which cannot be taught, they are inherent. It was always said at Morris's works at Merton that none of the workmen, even though they spent their whole time in doing it, could get the peculiarly beautiful shades that Morris did when he was dyeing.

When he took up printing in the last years of his life Morris declared, with his usual enthusiasm: "I wish I had been a printer from my mother's womb." But it was evident that he had not only been a printer, but a good many other things from that extremely early stage of existence. Most men do well if they make a name for themselves in one art, one form of creative craftsmanship. Morris was a poet and a prose romancer, a printer of such eminence that his *Chaucer* is one of the most noble printed books in the world; an illuminator; a designer of patterns of extraordinary inventiveness and grace; a weaver; the mainspring of a highly successful business; and finally a public man and politician—not on the safe and successful side but on the highly unpopular one. It is a remarkable record. We, looking back on it, do not fully realize its magnitude, for many of the things for which Morris struggled and fought are now accepted, but they were not accepted in his day.

16

Amid all these varied and ardent activities, particularly the pursuit of the new craft of dyeing which was to prove so important to the business, Morris's experiences in Iceland and among Icelandic literature were slowly coming to fruit. *Sigurd the Volsung* is probably the finest thing he ever did in poetry. Not necessarily the most perfect, certainly not the most enchanting, but the finest. And one reason for this judgement is because that epic reveals an inner man in Morris who has burst the sheath of his pleasant life; he is no longer leaning over the castle wall of romance and watching fair tourneys for a lady's smile. He has gone from the world in which the greatest grief was a lady's frown, and all tears were for love. He has left that world of romance and chivalry—underneath, unlike some of his circle, he had always suspected it was not a real world—and gone where there is older and starker sorrow; and through that long way round he was to come back to the griefs of his own day, the common griefs of poverty and hunger and lack of decent work, and all the ugliness that goes with poverty and ignorance.

But before *Sigurd the Volsung* was to appear Morris had produced two translations, one from the Icelandic, published as *Three Northern Love Stories*, and the other a verse translation of the *Æneid* of Virgil. These two works, one of a classic, and the other a translation from an almost unknown tongue, might seem considerable undertakings in themselves, but crammed in as they were between learning by practical experiment the art of dyeing—"I have found out and practised the art of weld-dyeing, the ancientest of yellow dyes, and the fastest"—running the expanding business, making lovely illuminated books with his own hand, they were to the amazing Topsy but the prelude to his major creative work of *Sigurd the Volsung*.

Of course it is easy enough to foresee the scornful shrug of the scholar to whom the translation of Virgil is a worthy life's work, at all this rich mixed activity. He would condemn Morris's bold effort without even looking at a single page. The difference between them was that Morris was not a scholar, never pretended to be one, but simply a man who had a feeling for one of the world's great tales and wished to share it with some of the people who could not read the language in which it was written. This, and his own pleasure in retelling the tale in his own words. It would disturb Morris not one whit to remember—if he did remember—the words of another and more learned translator who said: "A translator of Virgil into English verse, finds the road along which he has undertaken to travel strewn with the bleaching bones of unfortunate pilgrims who have preceded him."

The point which has always to be remembered about Morris is that he did things because he *liked* doing them, not because of any monetary or honorary rewards they might happen to bring him. This is so unusual that it is apt to be overlooked. He found the reward that mattered to him in the doing of the thing, whether it was a translation from another language, or a good hank of indigo yarn. His attitude is shown even in the comparatively small matter of pen or typewriter. Much as he wrote—there are twenty-four solid volumes of it—he could not endure or use the typewriter because of its mechanical quality. "Anything that gets between a man's hand and his work, you see, is more or less bad for him", he said. "There's a pleasant feel in the paper under one's hand and the pen between one's fingers that has its own part in the work done." He always wrote with a quill pen, because, as he declared, it was fuller in the hand for its weight and held the ink better. Perhaps also because Chaucer would have used a quill when he was writing the *Canterbury Tales*.

This close and intimate connection between the hand and the work is the secret of the true craftsman, who is happy whether poor or rich, so long as he works at the thing he can do and love to do. It is a secret almost completely lost in this industrialized civilization, as Morris knew and preached. There was only one activity in his life which he followed, because he felt it his duty, not because he liked it.

As might be expected, Morris's Virgil was a somewhat medieval one; his mind was definitely a romantic and Gothic mind, not classical. If scholars do not look to Morris's *Æneids*, many lovers of poetry can do so, and be grateful for the warmth which brings it nearer to their grasp.

By deep-rooted instinct Morris was not only more medieval than classical, he was a north man more than a south man, and in a sense discovered his homeland when he discovered Iceland. Therefore he held the *Volsunga Saga* above and alone among all other of the world's stories. "This is the Great Story of the north," he said, "which should be to our race what the Tale of Troy was to the Greeks."

About this story, Morris wrote some words which in

these days have almost an air of prophecy, and which also throw a strange light on some of the darker and rarely revealed places of his own heart:

It may be that the world shall worsen, that men shall grow afraid to change their life; that the world shall be weary itself, and sicken, and none but faint-hearts be left—who knows? So at any rate comes the end at last, and the Evil, bound for a while, is loose, and all nameless merciless horrors that on earth we figure by fire and earthquake and venom and raving. So comes the great strife; and like the kings and heroes that they have loved, here also must the Gods die, the Gods who made that strifeful imperfect earth, not blindly indeed, but foredoomed. One by one they extinguish for ever some dread and misery that all this time has brooded over life, and one by one, their work accomplished, they die; till at last the great destruction breaks out over all things, and the old earth and heavens are gone, and then a new heaven and earth. What goes on there? Who shall say, of us who know only of rest and peace by toil and strife? And what shall be our share in it? Well, sometimes we must needs think that we shall live again: yet if that were not, would it not be enough that we helped to make this unnameable glory, and lived not altogether deedless? Think of the joy we have in praising great men, and how we turn their stories over and over, and fashion their lives for our joy: and this also we ourselves may give to the world.

This seems to me pretty much the religion of the Northmen. I think one would be a happy man if one could hold it, in spite of the wild dreams and dreadful imaginings that hang about it here and there.

It was not often that Morris gave such a testament of his feelings as in those words.

17

Sigurd the Volsung starts off with glowing lines which are a somewhat deceptive opening to the grim and tragic tale that is to follow.

There was a dwelling of Kings ere the world was waxen old;
Dukes were the door-wards there, and the roofs were thatched
    with gold;
Earls were the wrights that wrought it, and silver nailed its
    doors;
Earls' wives were the weaving-women, queens' daughters
    strewed its floors,
And the masters of its song-craft were the mightiest men that
    last
The sails of the storm of battle adorn the bickering blast.
There dwelt men merry-hearted, and in hope exceeding great
Met the good days and the evil as they went the way of fate.

On its appearance *Sigurd* proved too tough a nut for the
taste of the general public. Where poetry was read at all,
it was the idyll and not the epic that was favoured. The
strange dark story of Sigurd's forebears was not suitable
for Victorian drawing-rooms, and where the heroes and
heroines of the Northern epic were known at all it was
veiled in the smoky clouds of Wagner's music and comfortably contained in the plump forms of Nordic operatic stars.
All this, as has been seen, was sheer desecration to Morris.

Sham trimmings were utterly repugnant to him in his
faithful adherence to the twelfth-century Icelandic original.
Too faithful, it may be admitted, for the unhewn story of
Sigmund and Signy and their son Sinfiotli, which fills the
first four books of Morris's poem, is apt to form a morass-
like barrier to the hopeful reader, and has no epic unity
with the story of Sigurd himself. But to those brave enough
to persevere through the first four books, they provide an
enormous darkling background, a landscape of storm and
steel. Morris himself regarded *Sigurd* as the greatest of his
works—or perhaps it would be truer to say that he felt it
was the greatest story he had ever told. And he rose to the
height of the great moment—it is impossible to forget
Gunnar in the pit of snakes singing his death-song till the
harp falls from his hand, or Brynhild when she has stabbed
herself claiming to share Sigurd's funeral pyre:

The bale for the dead is builded, it is wrought full wide on
    the plain,
It is raised for Earth's best Helper, and thereon is room for
    twain . . .
How then when the flames flare upward may I be left behind?
How then may the road he windeth be hard for my feet to find?

Or Gudrun when she cried before she leapt into the waves:

O sea, I stand before thee; and I who was Sigurd's wife!
By his brightness unforgotten I bid thee deliver my life
From the deeds and the longing of days, and the lack I have
    won of the earth,
And the wrong amended by wrong, and the bitter wrong of
    my birth.

But there was not much public acclamation of *Sigurd the
Volsung* on its first appearance. Morris had a short spasm
of ill-temper on the subject, but it soon passed, and he
was quickly immersed in his dyeing again and in further
Northern reading.

"I had been reading the Njala in the original before I
came here," he wrote from Leek, where he was engaged
in dyeing:

it is better even than I remembered; the style most solemn
(Dasent now and then uses a word too homely, I think, which
brings it down a little): all men's children in it, as always in
the best of the northern stories, so venerable to each other,
and so venerated: and the exceeding good temper of Gunnar
amidst his heroism, and the calm of Njal: and I don't know
anything more consoling or grander in all literature (to use a
beastly French word) than Gunnar's singing in his house under
the moon and the drifting clouds: or do you remember the
portents at Bergthorsknoll before the burning, and how Skarphedium takes them? Or Skarphedium's death; or how Flosi
pays the penalty for the Burning, never appealing against the
due and equal justice, but defending himself and his folk stoutly
against it at every step? What a glorious outcome of the worship
of Courage these stories are.

It will be seen how intimate and real these early Northern stories were to Morris; how completely he passed the barriers of race and time and took to his heart legends and tales that many people find cold and remote, if not repellent. This was a special quality in Morris's make-up and marked him as in some way different from his fellows. Rossetti, who as was to be expected, did not care for Northern Sagas, said once that he could not take any interest in a hero who had a dragon for a brother; whereupon Morris exclaimed hotly that he would rather have a dragon for a brother than a fool.

As was to be expected from Morris, any disappointment he felt at the general public indifference to his *Sigurd the Volsung*—which he felt himself was his best work—was soon buried under other jobs.

No doubt, all the same, a tribute which he received at this time to his eminence as a poet, his acknowledged eminence, must have been welcome. He was requested by Convocation to stand as a candidate for the vacant Chair of Poetry at Oxford, the last holder but one of which had been Matthew Arnold. It was a flattering offer; it would have linked him officially with that University for which he had a deep attachment, in spite of certain disagreements. But after carefully considering the matter Morris decided to decline.

"It seems to me", he wrote,

that the *practice* of any art rather narrows the artist in regard to the *theory* of it; and I think I come more than most men under this condemnation, so that though I have read a good deal and have a good memory, my knowledge is so limited and so ill-arranged that I can scarce call myself a man of letters: and moreover I have a peculiar ineptitude for expressing myself except in the one way that my gift lies. Also may I say without offence that I have a lurking doubt as to whether the Chair of Poetry is more than an ornamental one, and whether the Professor of a wholly incommunicable art is not rather in a false position.

Official positions, in any case, were not much to Morris's inclination; he was by instinct an individualist and a man who liked to follow his own road and find his own way of doing things.

18

Having declined the opportunity of becoming Oxford Professor of Poetry—which from the point of view of the University is regrettable, though it is a little difficult to imagine the impetuous and dye-stained Topsy in academic gowns—and finished his great epic, Morris almost unconsciously and without realizing it, was slowly stepping down from his Palace of Art into the public highway. Very properly he went forth as a valiant knight to rescue a lady in distress, and the lady was his long-loved mistress, Architecture.

From the 1860's to the beginning of the 1890's, perhaps more dreadful things were done against architecture in England than had ever been done before. The eighteenth century had some crimes on its conscience in regard to the "ruins" then so much admired. False ruins were erected in gentlemen's parks and draped with ivy and gloom—that was a folly of no particular importance. What was serious was the way in which the dilapidation of historic and ancient ruins was encouraged and the wicked destructiveness of parasitic ivy left unchecked, so that the ruins might induce a suitable "pensiveness" in the beholder. But all the eighteenth-century sins were as nothing to the deeds of mid-nineteenth century lack of taste and knowledge and cheap passion for neatness. Everything must be dressed up and tidy; varnish, pitchpine, and encaustic tiles must replace ancient oak and ashlar. "Restoration" was the soothing word under which many dark and irremediable deeds were done. Better still was it to pull down the old altogether and build something bright and new in the style of Queen Victoria's golden age. An Albert Memorial was obviously larger and more ornate than some shabby little stone Queen Eleanor Cross; therefore it was, equally obviously, better.

It was in the Cotswold country he was coming to know and love through his home at Kelmscott that Morris was first roused to definite action. In the autumn of 1876 he drove through Burford on the Windrush one day and was horrified to discover the vandalism that was going on in the name of "restoration"—"gammoning" became, in the course of time, the Morris family name for that process—in the beautiful old church there. By the shock this gave him he was roused to urge the necessity of forming some sort of public body to protect ancient buildings. Nothing much happened for some months, when in the spring of 1877 the proposed "restoration" of the noble Abbey Church of Tewkesbury brought Morris right out on the warpath. How much "the child is father of the man" is seen when remembering the little boy of eight who first beheld his heritage in Canterbury Cathedral, and the man in his middle forties who came out to do battle for Tewkesbury Abbey. To *The Athenaeum* Morris wrote a trumpet-sounding letter:

My eye just now caught the word "restoration" in the morning paper, and on looking closer, I saw that this time it is nothing less than the Minster of Tewkesbury that is to be destroyed by Sir Gilbert Scott. Is it altogether too late to do something to save it—it and whatever else of beautiful and historic is still left us on the sites of the ancient buildings we were once so famous for? Would it not be of some use once for all, and with the least delay possible, to set on foot an association for the purpose of watching over and protecting these relics, which, scanty as they are now become, are still wonderful treasures, all the more precious in this age of the world, when the newly invented study of living history is the chief joy of so many of our lives?

Your paper has so steadily and courageously opposed itself to these acts of barbarism which the modern architect, parson, and squire call "restoration", that it would be waste of words to enlarge here on the ruin that has been wrought by their hands; but, for the saving of what is left, I think I may write a word of encouragement, and say that you by no means stand alone in the matter, and that there are many thoughtful people who would be glad to sacrifice time, money, and comfort in defence of these ancient monuments: besides, though I admit that the architects are, with very few exceptions, hopeless, because interest, habit, and ignorance bind them, and that the clergy are hopeless, because their order, habit, and an ignorance yet grosser, bind them: still there must be many people whose ignorance is accidental rather than inveterate, whose good sense could surely be touched if it were clearly put to them that they were destroying what they, or more surely still, their sons and sons' sons, would one day fervently long for, and which no wealth or energy could ever buy again for them.

What I wish for, therefore, is that an association should be set on foot to keep a watch on old monuments, to protest against all "restoration" that means more than keeping out wind and weather, and, by all means, literary and other, to awaken a feeling that our ancient buildings are not mere ecclesiastical toys, but sacred monuments of the nation's growth and hope.

Had William Morris done nothing more notable in his life than write that letter he would have deserved remembrance by his country, for from it sprung within a month the Society for the Protection of Ancient Buildings—"Anti-Scrape" as Morris was to christen it. He was the first secretary, in spite of all the other jobs he had on his broad shoulders. He wrote an eloquent appeal and explanation of the Society's aims, and of the "enthusiasm, religious, historical, artistic", with which enlightened people were growing to regard the ancient buildings of England.

Among the first members of the Society was Thomas Carlyle. Cantankerous and contradictious in his well-known and admired manner, his principal reason for joining was because someone had apparently told him it was not worth supporting and because of his admiration for the work of Sir Christopher Wren, who was also, he said, glaring round at his listeners, not only a really great man, but "of extra-ordinary patience with fools".

Morris, of course, like Carlyle and other famous men, had his blind spots, and one of them was that he had no appreciation of the work of Wren and his successors. He was born too fundamentally Gothic and also too funda-mentally honest to pretend to an appreciation he did not feel. There was something in him always reaching back to starker days—in spite of his flowering love for beauty and rich colours and textures—to Iceland and the bleak Sagas, to a plain English landscape, even a little dreary, to a more simple and dangerous living. His musings were often in this manner:

> Not seldom I please myself with trying to realize the face of medieval England: the many chases and great woods, the stretches of common tillage and common pasture quite unen-closed; the rough husbandry of the tilled parts, the unimproved breeds of cattle, sheep, and swine, especially the latter, looking so strange to us; the strings of pack-horses along the bridle-roads, the scantiness of the wheel-roads, scarce any except those left by the Romans, and those made from monastery to monastery; the scarcity of bridges, and people using ferries instead, or fords when they could; the little towns well be-churched, often walled; the villages just where they are now (except for those that have nothing but the church left to tell of them), but better and more populous; their churches, some big and handsome, some small and curious, but all crowded with altars and furniture, and gay with pictures and ornament; the many religious houses, with their glorious architecture; the beautiful manor-houses, some of them castles once, and sur-vivals from an earlier period; some new and elegant; some out of all proportion small for the importance of their lords. How strange it would be to us if we could be landed in fourteenth-century England; unless we saw the crest of some familiar hill,

like that which yet bears upon it a symbol of an English tribe, and from which, looking down on the plain where Alfred was born, I once had many such ponderings.

When Morris gave his services and support he gave it generously, and in the following years several of his lectures and addresses were given for the benefit of the Society for the Protection of Ancient Buildings, and in these addresses he said some important things on the subject of architecture and the kindred arts in general so dear to him. A few sentences and paragraphs taken from these addresses give food for thought and help towards the understanding of Morris himself.

The following extracts come from "Architecture and History":

. . . it was the view of the benighted people of the Middle Ages that a man who bought, say, a hundredweight of cheese for twopence a pound at nine in the morning and sold it at eleven for threepence was not a specially useful citizen.

. . . the division of labour had so worked that instead of all workmen being artists, as they once were, they were divided into workmen who were not artists, and artists who were not workmen.

Under the old medieval conditions the unit of labour was a master craftsman who knew his business from beginning to end.

The picture-painters who were wont to show us, as through windows opened by them, the longings and lives of the saints and heroes, nay, the very heavens and City of God hanging over the earthly city of their love, were turned, what few of them were aught else than pretentious daubers, into courtly flatterers of ill-famed fine ladies and stupid supercilious lords. As for the architectural arts, what could you expect to get of them from a set of human machines, co-operating indeed, but only for speed and precision of production, and designed at best by pedants who despised the life of man, and at worst by mechanical drudges, little better in any way than the luckless workmen.

Here then is a strange contrast, which I must seriously

invite you to consider, between the craftsman of the Middle Ages and him of to-day. The medieval man sets to work at his own time, in his own house; probably makes his tool, instrument, or simple machine himself, even before he gets on to his web, or his lump of clay, or what not. What ornament there shall be on his finished work he himself determines, and his mind and hand designs it and carries it out; tradition, that is to say the minds and thoughts of all workmen gone before, this, in its concrete form of the custom of the crafts, does indeed guide and help him; otherwise he is free. Nor must we forget that even if he lives in a town, the fields and sweet country come close up to his house, and he at whiles occupies himself in working in them.

Believe me, it will not be possible for a small knot of cultivated people to keep alive an interest in the art and records of the past amidst the present conditions of a sordid and heart-breaking struggle for the many, and a languid sauntering through life for the few. But when society is so reconstituted that all citizens will have a chance of leading a life made up of due leisure and reasonable work, then will all society, and not our society only, resolve to protect ancient buildings from all damage, wanton or accidental, for then at last they will begin to understand that they are part of their present lives and part of themselves. That will come when the time is ripe for it; for at present even if they knew of their loss they could not prevent it, since they are living in a state of war, that is to say, of blind waste.

This lecture was given in July 1884.
Three years earlier Morris had addressed the potters of Burslem on "Art and the Beauty of the Earth", and it was in this lecture that he made his fundamental statement:

Time was when everybody that made anything made a work of art besides a useful piece of goods, *and it gave them pleasure to make it*. That is an assertion from which nothing can drive me; whatever I doubt, I have no doubt of that. And, sirs, if there is anything in the business of my life worth doing, if I have any worthy aspiration, it is the hope that I may help to bring about the day when we shall be able to say, So it was once, so it is now.

He emphasized the need of the workman doing the whole job:

I know by experience that the making of design after design —mere diagrams, mind you—without oneself executing them, is a great strain upon the mind. It is necessary, unless all workmen of all grades are to be permanently degraded into machines, that the hand should rest the mind as well as the mind the hand. And I say that this is the kind of work which the world has lost, supplying its place with the work which is the result of the division of labour.

Morris's last lecture for the Society for the Protection of Ancient Buildings was in 1893, and was concerned with the defence of Westminster Abbey against proposed "restoration". He did not spare his comments on the misfortunes of the great Abbey Church, which

being situated in the centre of government of this country, has not enjoyed the advantages of boorish neglect which have left so much of interest in medieval buildings in remoter parts of the country.

He denounces the hideous monumental sculpture with which the Abbey is crowded, and works in a few of the other things he dislikes:

The heavy hand of the academical classical architect has been more or less all over the building outside. The north transept, which in the time of Hollar, if one may judge from his curious nondescript engraving, was in a genuine condition, though possibly needing repair greatly, was reduced to the due commonplace ugliness which was then thought to be impressively respectable; the western towers omitted by the medieval builders were supplied in the same style, having been probably designed by Wren and carried out by Hawksmoor, and remain in good condition as monuments of the incapacity of seventeenth- and eighteenth-century architects to understand the work of their forefathers; and perhaps one might say that they furnish a wholesome lesson to future ages not to attempt the imitation of a past epoch of art. If the architect or architects of those towers had left the Gothic alone and built the new towers in the queer style of driven-into-a-corner classic, which is that of the city church towers of or about that date, they would certainly not have jarred our sense of congruity so much as the quasi-Gothic existing ones do, and also, which is a great point, they would not have been so ugly.

19

Morris was so naturally at home in the ages when great architecture was a living art that it seems wrong in many ways to drag him into the modern world, especially into the modern political world, whose atmosphere, squabbles, and preoccupations can never have been anything but brutal to him. Since he was a young man he had lived and worked with artists, saved from any harassing struggle with the world by the possession of a liberal income. This enabled him, unlike the majority of less fortunate men, to work hard and long—and his capacity for work was phenomenal—at all the things he cared about. While he was young and the world very fair he had fallen into love and married a girl so beautiful that she was like a princess —a rather forlorn princess—out of a fairy-tale. He had a wife, an ancient and lovely home, and two delightful daughters. It might have seemed that Morris's future was to be increasing prosperity and content, surrounded by the things he knew were beautiful and believed necessary to his life, more and more aloof from the cries and struggles and ugliness of the world.

But suddenly his life swung round from the placid direction it seemed to be taking; the Thames so fresh and peaceful at Kelmscott, was less clean and a good deal less peaceful at the Pool, cries and noise and trouble sounded on the wind.

The first cry to come to Morris's ears might be called a dumb cry, a silent cry, which yet sounded strongly in his mind—the cry of the buildings which had survived so many centuries, gently crumbling here and there under weather and human usage, suddenly assaulted by "gammoning". Morris heard that cry.

Then another and more agonized and urgent cry broke on his ears from mid-Europe. This was the cry of the Turkish atrocities in Bulgaria; so far, as it might seem, outside Morris's world. Few would have blamed him if he had felt it was no affair of his; he was an artist and a poet, not a politician or a man of affairs. Few of his fellow artists felt called upon to do anything about it—why should Morris? But he did.

Into all the details of that business and the formation of the Eastern Question Association it is fortunately unnecessary to go at this distance of time. The European pot has boiled over so many times and with such terrible results since then. The interesting thing to emphasize in this connection is that it reveals an entirely new aspect of Morris. He stands forth with something of the candid vigour of that other William whose surname was Cobbett —an angry Englishman with a clenched fist and a pugnacious eye. His words might well have come out of the very mouth of Cobbett. "Who are they that are leading us into war?" Morris asked,

> Greedy gamblers on the Stock Exchange, idle officers of the army and navy (poor fellows!), worn-out mockers of the clubs, desperate purveyors of exciting war-news for the comfortable breakfast-tables of those who have nothing to lose by war; and lastly, in the place of honour, the Tory Rump, that we fools, weary of peace, reason, and justice, chose at the last election to represent us. Shame and double shame, if we march under such leadership as this in an unjust war against a people who are not our enemies, against Europe, against freedom, against nature, against the hope of the world.

This is not the voice, these are not the words of "an idle singer of an empty day", that singularly unfortunate line for so long regarded as a self-portrait of the writer. The last epithet that could ever be applied to Morris was that of "idle". The only "idle" pursuit in which he ever indulged (if such a word may be applied to an angler) was that of fishing, and from all accounts he followed this art and mystery with such vigour that there was little peace and no idleness connected with it. And as his days were never idle so were they never empty, except in so far as, like all imaginative people, he found a golden quality in past time, and felt that a fourteenth-century day would fill his need better than did those of the mid-nineteenth century.

But there is one thing which both the admirers and the belittlers of William Morris are apt to forget: he was very much an Englishman. As English as Cobbett, though it was a matter on which he was less vocal than Cobbett. But had those two met they would have understood each other, even though they rode on different roads. Morris had a strong admiration for the *Rural Rides* and knew them well. He responded naturally to Cobbett's rich vehemence: his own matched it. But in regard to his feeling for his country he did not in general find himself compelled to say much about it, any more than he talked about his feelings for his wife. It is inherent and implicit in all he wrote and said about the art and history of England, and his dread of the day he felt was coming when "all the old is gone, and history has become a book from which the pictures have been torn".

But it was not only the high romantic England that appealed to him; he liked it broad and plain as well. In which again he was at one with Cobbett. George Borrow was another writer he admired and read constantly, and also Surtees, which on the face of it was an odd taste in him. As Mackail has said:

> In a man who never hunted, who seldom even rode, and to whom the life of a country house in the hunting season was not merely alien but odious, this preference must remain something of an unexplained mystery.

But Morris regaled his friends with the doings of Mr.
Jorrocks in season and out. He professed that Surtees was
as good as Dickens, and for Dickens he had a hearty and
most English devotion. Joe Gargary and Mr. Boffin were
his chosen companions. The "Morning, morning!" of Mr.
Boffin, and Joe Gargary's "Wot larks" were forms of
address that were constantly upon his lips. When he
wanted to express disapproval his favourite expression was
that of Mr. F.'s aunt: "Bring him forrard, and I'll chuck
him out o' winder."

His own manners and ways had a kind of natural
Dickensian quality. He swore fluently and frequently; it
was a sort of escape valve for some of his superfluous energy,
and he had a way of growling to himself which he called
"talking to nobody in particular".

The story is told of him lunching with a friend at the
Cock Tavern in Fleet Street; the "sanded floor and quaint
old-fashioned settees" appealed to him. The following day
the same friend was lunching there again by himself, and
the waiter came up to him and said: "That was a loudish
gent a-lunching with you yesterday, sir. I thought once
you was coming to blows." The waiter was probably not
enlightened as to the subject of the heated discussion,
which was Elizabethan dramatists. The "loudish gent"
had been abusing Cyril Tourneur.

When Morris was roused, whether it was over a Tudor
dramatist, or the Bulgarian horrors and the anti-Russian
warmongers, he spoke out with characteristic vehemence.
His own immediate circle were used to this when it
was applied to artistic questions or "Anti-Scrape", but
when he turned this passionate feeling on to political
matters, when he entered the arena of public affairs,
they were disturbed and startled. But there was worse
to come.

20

Morris's rebellious locks have been crowned with a kind of pre-Raphaelite wreath. As a young man he had been the model of his fellow artists for Tristram, Lancelot, the Angel Gabriel, or any of the Three Kings. He stood for anyone who was romantic, beautiful, and remote from the commonplace world of everyday. He was painted by Watts as himself, but Watts turned him into a kind of seer. He was constantly garbed in medieval armour. Though it is true when the armour proved a little tight he extricated himself with a rich violence of language, but his friends smiled and said: Oh, it was only one of Topsy's ways. Morris was by nature singularly unself-conscious—he did not mind wearing wreaths and chain-mail, so long as it did not interfere with his pursuits. The only thing he really objected to was a top-hat, which for a time he had to wear at the meetings of some City Company. When he no longer had to attend these meetings he came home, and solemnly, with great satisfaction, sat down on his tall silk hat. He must have looked extremely funny in it— "with all that hair, too", as Browning said.

But though Morris's closest and oldest friend, Burne-Jones, did not properly live in this world at all, Morris himself had deep roots growing in quite ordinary soil— not in any Fata Morgana Country at all. His head was splendid and romantic, but his stocky body and short legs, his rolling walk, gave him a marked seafaring look, and it is not surprising that a sailor once stepped up to him and said: "Beg pardon, sir, but was you once Captain of the *Skylark*?" Morris was thoroughly pleased by this little encounter.

As he grew older and wiser—for he was one of the rare people who continued to grow all his life—he had no wish to shut himself away from the light of common day, to live, as had been his early dream, in a Brotherhood cut off

THE OLDER MORRIS.

from the world. He had seen something of the results of living exclusively for "art" in several of his associates, and his sturdy common sense did not think them particularly wholesome. He wanted and needed beauty, and never all his life long gave up this proper requirement of human life. No one more fully than Morris could say with Robert Bridges:

> I love all beauteous things,
> I seek and adore them;
> God hath no better praise,
> And man in his hasty days
> Is honoured for them.
> I too will something make
> And joy in the making.

But he would not pay a fantastic price for this beauty. He ceased to think—if he ever had thought so—that it belonged to the few who, in his day, cared for it. His historic imagination and knowledge told him that in the past beauty had not been shut up in museums and rich men's houses, but had been the ordinary attribute of everyday living—so normal that every stone-mason who carved a pillar, every smith who wrought an iron lock or sanctuary-knocker, every carpenter who made a livery cupboard or a bit of panelling, made a thing of beauty. Nobody knows who planned and built the old village churches, because it was regarded as so natural and normal a thing and was done by so many hands, that it was anonymous, and yet personal to all. If a bridge, a barn, or a dovecote was needed, it was built, and that was all there was to it. It is us of a so much later generation who marvel at the barn at Great Coxwell—as Morris did, it was one of his particular joys—or a pigeon house like a Norman Keep in some remote farmyard. To the builders of such things they were just simple everyday jobs.

With things like these in his mind Morris looked at what he saw around him at Turnham Green and at

Hammersmith, and felt quite naturally that something was very wrong. But—and this is where he swung quite away from the friends and the tendencies of his whole life up to this period—he did not say there was nothing he could do about it, that he was not responsible; that he had better stick to his own affairs. He said none of these things because he was fundamentally honest. New thoughts, new convictions, had come into his mind, and they forced him into new ways.

In the year 1881 he said this:

As I sit at my work at home which is at Hammersmith, close to the river, I often hear some of that ruffianism go past the window of which a good deal has been said in the papers of late, and has been said before at recurring periods. As I hear the yells and shrieks and all the degradation cast on the glorious tongue of Shakespeare and Milton, as I see the brutal reckless faces and figures go past me, it rouses the recklessness and brutality in me also, and fierce wrath takes possession of me, till I remember, as I hope I mostly do, that it was my good luck only of being born respectable and rich, that has put me on this side of the window among delightful books and lovely works of art, and not on the other side, in the empty street, the drink-steeped liquor shops, the foul and degraded lodgings. What words can say what all that means? . . . I know by my own feelings and desires what these men want, what would have saved them from this lowest depth of savagery: employment which would foster their self-respect and win the praise and sympathy of their fellows, and dwellings which they could come to with pleasure, surroundings which would soothe and elevate them; reasonable labour, reasonable rest . . . The land we live in is not very big either in actual acreage or in scale of fashion, but I think it is not our natural love for it only that makes us think it as fit as any land for the peaceful dwellings of serious men. Our fathers have shown us that if it could otherwise be doubted, I say, without fear of contradiction, that no dwelling of men has ever been sweeter or pleasanter than an ancient English house; but our fathers treated our lovely land well, and we have treated it ill.

At another time he wrote, almost with a touch of prophecy:

> Suppose people lived in little communities among gardens and green fields, so that you could be in the country in five minutes' walk, and had few wants, almost no furniture, for instance, and no servants, and studied the (difficult) arts of enjoying life, and finding out what they really wanted: then I think one might hope civilization had really begun. But as it is, the best thing one can wish for this country at least is, meseems, some great and tragical circumstances, so that if they cannot have a pleasant life, which is what one means by civilization, they may at least have a history and something to think of.

Such thoughts and ideas flow for some time under the visible streams of life before they come to the surface. Morris's socialism was not so much a conversion as a discovery that he had been a socialist all the time. Perhaps most conversions are like that—a silent growth, whose only point of surprise is the point where it emerges to the surface.

It was a surprise to his friends—indeed, a shock, for in few, if any, of them was there any similar growth to meet it. There can be no doubt that Morris felt this sudden isolation, after all the comradeship and admiration he had enjoyed. But he had a nature well fitted to stand up to it, because things, ideas, had always been in the forefront of his life, and he was not fundamentally dependent upon persons.

Morris's first struggles with the difficulties and jealousies and dishonesties of the political scene went hard with him. He had no diplomatic skill, and no evasive arts; he took the full force of all blows and gave back as good as he might. This, combined with the immense amount of hard work he was putting in at dyeing, and the beginning of the firm's tapestry weaving, began to tell upon his health. In the spring of 1878 he fell ill with a bad attack of rheumatic fever, his old enemy. When partially recovered he went out to Italy to join his wife and daughters, who had

been there since the previous November, but much of
the expected pleasure was lost because of his health.   He
fainted on one occasion, and had to be carried on a man's
back, "like a Guy Fawkes". This illness left its traces with
him for the rest of his life. He was only in his middle
forties, but he had always driven himself hard—his super-
abundant energies would hardly let him sit still, even
through a meal—he must get up and walk about, even
if only to look out of the window. The only thing that
could really keep him still was sleep—in which he was like
a child.

Italy, in any case, never appealed to him in the same
way, or to the same extent, as some other foreign countries,
and it is partly that and partly the effects of his illness
which gives an autumnal touch to a letter he wrote from
there:

Many times I think of the first time I ever went abroad, and
to Rouen, and what a wonder of glory that was to me when
I first came upon the front of the cathedral rising above the
flower-market. It scarcely happens to me like that now, at
least not with man's work, though whiles it does with bits of
the great world, like the Garda Lake the other day, or unexpected sudden sights of the mountains. Even the inside of
St. Mark's gave one rather deep satisfaction, and not for the
eyes, than that strange exaltation of spirits, which I remember
of old in France, and which the mountains give me yet.

I don't think this is wholly because I am grown older, but
because I really have had more sympathy with the North from
the first in spite of all the faults of its work. Let me confess it
and be hanged: with the later work of Southern Europe I am
quite out of sympathy. In spite of its magnificent power and
energy I feel it as an enemy, and this much more in Italy,
where there is such a mass of it, than elsewhere. Yes, and even
in these magnificent and wonderful towns I long rather for
the heap of grey stones with a grey roof that we call a home
north-away.

In other words, Kelmscott Manor.

It was in the autumn of the same year as his visit to Italy that Morris settled down in his last London home, Kelmscott House, Hammersmith. It shows how little he allowed any memory of past illness to interfere with his pursuits, that as soon as he moved into Kelmscott House he had a tapestry-loom set up in his bedroom, and on it he wove his first complete tapestry, the Cabbage and Vine. To it he devoted 516 working hours in four months—all this out of his "leisure" time, being otherwise fully occupied with his business and his increasing interest in socialism.

He not only had the loom in his bedroom, but the stables and coach-house at Kelmscott House were converted into a weaving-shed, and there were produced the beautiful "Hammersmith" carpets and rugs, so called from the place of their origin. This long weaving-shed, when the work was taken elsewhere, eventually became the meeting-place of the Hammersmith socialists.

The house Morris loved with his soul was Kelmscott Manor, but he had a good hearty liking for his workaday Hammersmith home. In certain moods he felt that he was a town-bird, that he had soot on his feathers, like the London sparrows. "Lord bless us," he wrote, "how nice it will be when I can get back to my little patterns and dyeing, and the dear warp and weft at Hammersmith."

It was not only that Hammersmith meant work—always his first and fundamental love—and Kelmscott on the Upper Thames leisure, so far as he ever indulged in leisure. It was a deeper feeling growing in him that in order to accomplish some of the things he began to feel he must do, sacrifice was necessary. Perhaps he had known too good a life, had too much of the things he wished and delighted in? From Kelmscott Manor he wrote on an autumn evening:

I am sitting now, 10 p.m., in the tapestry room, the moon rising red through the east-wind haze, and a cow lowing over the fields. I have been feeling chastened by many thoughts, and the beauty and quietness of the surroundings, which later, as I hinted, I am, as it were, beginning to take leave of. That leave-taking will, I must confess, though you may think it fantastic, seem a long step towards saying good night to the world.

That lovely grey old house, that tapestry room, still exist very much as Morris knew them. Who knows but that, as the tinted autumn moon rises and shines into those stone-mullioned windows, some memory, some emanation of Morris in that solemn mood, troubled and conscious of the "still, sad music of humanity" set in the peace of night and nature, may not hover there?

21

The seeds of socialism were growing in Morris's mind, but clear and distinct action did not come till the decade of 1880. The time before was filled in with plenty of hard work and plenty of new schemes. The show-rooms of the firm were now established at the shop in Oxford Street so long familiar, till it finally moved to the fine premises in Hanover Square which lacked all contact with Morris himself. Queen Square, with oddments of stabling at Hammersmith, still produced the beautiful things that were to be seen and sold in Oxford Street. With the increasing business it was plain this could hardly continue.

Morris at this time was doubly busy with plans and schemes for making things because he had no plans for making poetry. For so long the two—poetry, and the crafts of his hands—had gone on together, that the idleness of his pen gave him a kind of pain. There was something missing from his life, which, in a way, was just as necessary to him as his breakfast. "The verse would come easy enough if I had only a subject which would fill my heart and mind," he wrote towards the end of 1879, "but to

KELMSCOTT MANOR: THE GREEN ROOM.

write verse for the sake of writing is a crime in a man of my years and experience."

Actually, though he did not know it when he said that he had finished writing poetry, *Sigurd the Volsung* was his poetic swan-song. He was to write much more, but it was to be in another manner altogether.

This failure of his poetic inspiration—for it must have been that, or he would have found his "subject"—drove him with more urgency into the affairs of the business. It was Morris's peculiarity to like always to have two, if not three, pursuits in hand together. The new craft of carpet-making, which he had taken on, begun so simply in the stables of his house at Hammersmith, progressed so well that in the early summer of 1880 there was an exhibition of them, these carpets being "an attempt", wrote Morris, in the circular issued by the firm, "to make England independent of the East for carpets which may claim to be considered works of art".

"We believe", Morris goes on:

> that the time has come for someone or other to make that attempt, unless the civilized world is prepared to do without the art of carpet-making at its best: for it is a lamentable fact that, just when we of the west are beginning to understand and admire the art of the East, that art is fading away, nor in any branch has the deterioration been more marked than in carpet-making . . . It seems to us, therefore, that for the future, we peoples of the West must make our own hand-made carpets, if we are to have any worth the labour and money such things cost; and that these, while they should equal the Eastern ones as nearly as maybe in materials and durability, should by no means imitate them in design, but show them-selves obviously to be the outcome of modern and Western ideas, guided by those principles that underlie all architectural art in common.

Morris had a great feeling for beautiful carpets, and he became an acknowledged authority on the subject. The collections at the South Kensington Museum owe much to his advice and help. The Royal School of Art Needle-work also owed him much. With his own hands he could do lovely embroideries, as well as design them, and when he took up the craft of dyeing silks, he produced colours that no other living person could equal. One of his most gifted embroidery pupils, Miss Holiday, has said:

> He actually did create new colours; then in his amethysts and golds and green, they were different to anything I have ever seen; he used to get a marvellous play of colour into them. The amethyst had flushings of red; and his gold (our special sort), when spread out in the large rich hanks, looked like a sunset sky. When he got an unusually fine piece of colour he would send it off to me or keep it for me; when he ceased to dye with his own hands I soon felt the difference. The colours themselves became perfectly level, and had a monotonous look; the very lustre of the silk was less beautiful. When I complained, he said: "Yes, they have grown too clever at it—of course it means they don't love colour, or they would do it."

Of course what it really meant was that they lacked just that touch of genius which Morris brought to all the things he did. He was completely unconscious of this—would scoff at any suggestion that it was unusual; he believed that anybody could do the same if they wanted to do so. He would have agreed with the idea of Eric Gill that an artist was not a special kind of man, but that every man was a special kind of artist.

22

Morris's personal and private affairs were, taken all round, singularly fortunate. Without giving away too much of his inner self—which he only did to very few, and with difficulty—he had many friends and devoted adherents and admirers, as well as plenty of people who were always joyfully wondering what Topsy would do next. He was on the friendliest terms with his mother. There is a portrait of her taken in 1879, showing what a fine firm old face she had, in many ways like her son's in certain masculine qualities, in spite of the Victorian old lady's garb of stiff black silk gown, looped gold watch chain, lace cap and lace lappets. The white curls peeping from the cap are as thick and abundant as Topsy's own. In spite of the conventions of her period, which stretched back almost to the beginning of the nineteenth century, old Mrs. Morris understood her son. So Morris was fortunate in his mother.

His friendship with Ned Burne-Jones, begun at Oxford, was never broken, and this was the friendship which of all others mattered most in both their lives. Then he had married young, the only woman with whom he seems to have ever been in love, who must have been a perpetual and romantic joy to his beauty-loving eyes, and who, if in character somewhat negative, appears to have been gentle and malleable enough to fit in with his needs. There are few stories and anecdotes about her—she was evidently content to be the background, the very decorative background, to a great man. She had apparently endless patience in sitting still to be painted, and in sitting still while she was read aloud to—Morris read all his poems aloud to her. The only activity of hers that is generally mentioned is that of embroidery. The only way in which she stands apart from her husband is the fact that when Morris had completely broken with Rossetti, and freed himself from that octopus clutch, Jane Morris continued to visit him at intervals.

It is evident from what May Morris says about him in her introductions to her father's *Collected Works*, that he was a delightful and exciting kind of parent. He would be. He was full of a high adventurous kind of spirits, he liked a lark, and more than all he was always making things— tangible, visible things, which to the young are so enchanting and satisfactory. It is very easy to see "the littles", as he called them, trotting after their father and keeping a close and catlike eye upon his every movement, whether he was preparing to fish for gudgeon or illuminating on vellum. His daughter May, at any rate, shared his passion for everything to do with water—"messing about in boats"—and the art of angling. She even prepared his unpleasant bait without a qualm. Whenever he was caught in the river floods at Kelmscott, or fell out of a leaky boat, he always regretted if May was not with him to share in these joyful discomforts.

His elder girl, Jane Alice, called Jenny, was a little apart. She was very serious and clever. If May was his good comrade, Jenny was his love. Especially after her illness. It was through Jenny that the poignancy of love, the anguish of it, struck at last at Morris. It is doubtful if he had experienced it till epilepsy smote Jenny. One of his friends once said that Jenny was the only person who brought out his hidden tenderness, the only person he loved with pain. Through her attacks, her resulting delicacy, Morris endured the keenest suffering of his life. The letters he wrote to her when they were apart have a touch of yearning and fear. In the ordinary way Morris was a poor letter-writer, stiff and rather commonplace. It was not one of the arts he cultivated.

He did not cultivate manners either. He was brusque and a little rough—in spite of all the ideas of medieval chivalry he imbibed in his youth he had little gallantry towards women. It is somewhat difficult to avoid the idea that he preferred them as a wall decoration in paint or tapestry, to actually present in the flesh, when he might be forced to talk to them. He hated social functions. "I won't waste a day out of my precious life in grinning a company grin," he once said.

Apart from the women of his own household, the only women he comfortably tolerated were those who were a kind of extension of his own household, like Burne-Jones's wife and daughter (to whom he gave many beautiful specimens of his own handiwork) and a few old friends whom he had known a long time. A woman had little chance of obtaining his notice, unless she were vouched for, as it were, by some man who was one of his friends. In his *Diaries*, Wilfrid Scawen Blunt says of Morris:

He had little patience with fools, and the prettiest woman in the world could not seduce him into listening to nonsense if there was nothing of fact behind it. His time was too precious to waste on them: and the fine ladies who affected artistic tastes in his company without real knowledge put him straightaway to flight. To such he was rude and repellent.

To set against this Blount also says farther on:

He was generous and open-handed in his dealings, and I fancy did many kindnesses in a money way for people in distress, but he fashed himself for no man and for no woman. The truth is he would not give an hour of his *time* to anyone, he held it to be too valuable.

Perhaps this somewhat marked masculinity of his, the slightly emphasized roughness and robustness, was a half-conscious revolt against the morbid strain, the too-emphasized cult of beauty, of the Pre-Raphaelites who so deeply influenced Morris's youth. Rossetti's influence in reverse, as it were. A violent nature like that of Morris is apt to extremes. "Of all men I ever heard of I have the strongest will for good and ill", said Morris when he was young, dramatizing himself as the young do, yet with truth in it too;

I could soon find out whether a thing were possible or not for me: then if it were not, I threw it away for ever, never thought of it again, no regrets, no longing for that, it was past and over to me; but, if it were possible and I made up my mind to do it, then and there I began it, turning neither to the right hand nor to the left hand till it was done. So I did with all things I set my hand to.

Time was always a thing he regarded as of incalculable value, because he always could see every bit of time that life might give him as filled with work that he longed to do.

So he had no time for "social" life. But there was a wholesome small boy streak in his character that prevented him
becoming too much the worker-bee. Any suggestion of
a river-holiday, picnic, fishing, was enough to make him
cast off industry, and take to the Thames.

The Morris family, assisted by close friends and
colleagues like the Burne-Joneses and the De Morgans,
made epic water-journeys from Kelmscott House at
Hammersmith to Kelmscott Manor, and many amusing
accounts of their adventures on these aquatic pilgrimages
remain. Morris's part ranges from that of the bear to the
schoolboy, according to the nature of the person describing the scene. Violet Hunt is somewhat acid—she was
not particularly fond of Morris, his bluntness offended her
youthful touchiness. In an article she once wrote for the
London Mercury, she described vividly how she watched one
of those pilgrimages up the Thames, with the "Hector of
Hammersmith", as she called Morris, in the first boat:

> Standing up and shouting indecorously worded advice to the
> other boat was the man who loved a battle shout better than
> a symphony, the Defender of Guenevere and of Gudrun,
> straddling, legs apart in the boat as erstwhile waggishly
> depicted by his pals on the ceiling of the Oxford Union, the
> Viking in the blue byrnie . . . Behind him, sitting up very
> stiffly, as a weary queen on her dais of turkey-red cushions,
> was the historic Janey.

A naturally warmer and more intimate account of these
river expeditions is given by Morris's younger daughter in
her remembrances of that time.

"The Ark" was the very suitable name given to the
craft in which the first journey up river was taken in
the summer of 1880. Morris described her as a boat with
a kind of omnibus on board, in which there was not very
much room. "Still what joy (to a little mind)", he went
on, "to see the landscape out of a square pane of glass, and
to sleep a-nights with the stream rushing two inches past

one's ear. Then after all there is the romance of the bank, and outside the boat the world is wide."

At times his two homes worried him, when he was at one there always seemed a reason why he should be at the other. "More and more I think people ought to live in one place—pilgrimages excepted."

The first "Ark" expedition was a long slow progress, stopping at various famous places such as Windsor and Eton on the way, which Morris admitted, with a somewhat naïve astonishment, were not as bad as he expected. He was cook to the expedition, a job which he enjoyed and did extremely well, "appearing", he said, "like the high priest at the critical moment, pot in hand".

The popular and populous parts of the Thames did not appeal to Morris, but when he was in Marlow in the summer dusk, having taken his wife and daughters to sleep at an inn there, he "looked up the street, and saw the streamers of the Northern Lights flickering all across that part of the sky, just as I saw them in '71 (and not since) in the harbour of Thorshaven: it was very mysterious and almost frightening to see them over the summer leafage so unexpectedly".

He was glad when they reached "the Thames, that is the Thames amidst the down-like country". And so he came by water to Oxford, where, strangely enough, he had only been three times since his 'Varsity days.

The last stages of the journey were reached as they came to Radcot, with its steep-shouldered medieval bridge, one of the oldest on the Thames, which Morris loved. "Night fell on us", he said in his account of this pilgrimage,

long before we got to Radcot, and we fastened a lantern to the prow of our boat, after we had with much difficulty, got our boats through Radcot Bridge. Charles was waiting us with a lantern at our bridge by the corner at 10 p.m., and presently the ancient house had me in its arms again.

Janey Morris had gone on before them by train from

Oxford, so that when the voyagers arrived in the summer evening the windows of Kelmscott Manor were all softly shining by lamplight for its master's return. That burly man, approaching fifty, obscurely troubled by ideas that were clutching at him, as he opened the narrow door in the grey wall, and saw the stars above the grey roof of his house and the candle-shine in its windows, perhaps breathed in his heart the words he was later to write down: "O me! O me! How I love the earth and the seasons, and the weather, and all things that deal with it, and all that grows out of it—as this has done!'

23

This river trip was repeated the following summer—Morris himself, with a touch of pessimism, being doubtful of the wisdom of repeating a successful adventure. But it came off all right this second time as well, for "according to my recollection", said William De Morgan, "we none of us stopped laughing all the way". One of his remembrances is of Morris sitting cooking the dinner inside the house-boat, "with the window closed to keep the wind off the spirit lamp, and ourselves outside looking at him through the glass".

Morris not only cooked the dinner, but when the party sat in a circle on the river bank eating it he kept them quiet by telling them an Icelandic or other story. Another of his amusements was detection of the misdemeanours of the Thames Conservancy.

Having reached Kelmscott by water in that second summer of 1881, Morris observed all that was going on in the countryside with minute interest, and tramped about the surrounding regions, studying architecture from the Roman villa to the Gothic church and barn, and the lovely Cotswold villages, with an increasing and deepening sense of the meaning and importance of these things. Some of those feelings he expressed in an address he gave at Burslem:

"I myself", he said,

am just fresh from an out-of-the-way part of the country near the end of the navigable Thames, where within a radius of five miles are some half-dozen tiny village churches, every one of which is a beautiful work of art. These are the works of the Thames-side country bumpkins, as you would call us—nothing grander than that. If the same sort of people were to design and build them now, they could not build anything better than the ordinary little plain nonconformist chapels that one sees scattered about new neighbourhoods. That is what they correspond with, not an architect-designed new Gothic church. The more you study architecture, the more certain you will become that I am right in this, and that what we have left us of earlier art was made by the unhelped people. Neither will you fail to see that it was made intelligently and with pleasure.

That last word brings me to a point so important that at the risk of getting wearisome, I must add it to my old sentence and repeat the whole. Time was when everybody that made anything made a work of art besides a useful piece of goods, *and it gave them pleasure to make it*. Whatever I doubt, I have no doubt of that.

I know that in those days life was often rough and evil enough, beset by violence, superstition, ignorance, slavery: yet sorely as poor folks needed a solace, they did not altogether lack one, and that solace was pleasure in their work. Much as the world has won since then, I do not think it has won for all men such perfect happiness that we can afford to cast aside any solace that nature holds out to us, or must we ever be casting out one devil by another? Shall we never make a push to get rid of the whole pack of them at once?

In the first years of the 1880's Morris's ethical convictions on the subject of work and art and morality—the convictions of the "poetic upholsterer" as one of his detractors had called him—were slowly taking definite form. Morris was no man to brood upon his convictions

6

—he had to do something about it. In a depressed mood he wrote:

I have of late been somewhat melancholy (rather too strong a word, but I don't know another), not so much so as not to enjoy life in a way, but just so much as a man of middle-age who has met with rubs (though less than his share of them) may sometimes be allowed to be.

The confused and wandering words show a certain childish puzzling at his own depression. But it is one of the things which must always be remembered about Morris, that depression was continually lurking round the corner with him. That was not the outward impression he gave, sturdily built, violent in speech and in action, always busy about something. "A rock of defence to us all, and a castle on the top of it, and a banner on the top of that", as Burne-Jones had said of him in his youth. But even in his youth the melancholy was there, and Morris knew it— knew that in some strange and uncomfortable way he was not in his right world, and he fought this knowledge and this obscure unhappiness by his mad passion for work, for constantly being occupied in hand and brain, with both hand and brain together, if possible, as in weaving and composing verse at the same time. It was self-protection, even if he did not know it. In his mind he was a dreamer, but a dreamer who must always be doing, and the need increased upon him, not lessened, as he grew older. He may have felt, as people sometimes do, that he was not destined to old age. "For happy folk", he said in his *Earthly Paradise*, "no time can pass too slow, because they die."

It is impossible to look at his many photographs—and his portrait was taken not only by the ordinary commercial photographer, but by people so eminent as Frederick Hollyar and Emery Walker—and think that his is the face of a happy man. Apart from the remote and "inexpressive eyes" the lines on the forehead are troubled lines, the frown is sharp, the lift and droop of the brows is a puzzled one. The happiest of his photographs is one taken in his study at Hammersmith by Halliday Sparling, where he is seated at his table writing, his curly hair and beard showing almost white against the dark background of books and furniture—he looks comfortable and absorbed in what he is doing. But the serenity of this picture is unusual. The "poetic upholsterer" had experienced a good deal more than that description would suggest, and always he lived hard, cramming all he could into the hours. "To me", as he once said, "every day begins and ends a year."

24

As an "upholsterer" Morris at this time of his life was more flourishing than ever before. Even Queen Victoria —whose conception of beauty was certainly very different from Morris's: indeed, all his efforts had been directed against the Victorian home in its material aspect—was constrained to set the seal of her approval upon his work. In this connection it is funny to recall that Morris, as a youth of seventeen, went to see that Victorian Wonder of the World, that glittering seal set upon peace and prosperity, the Great Exhibition of 1851, and having arrived there, sat down and declined to look at it, declaring that the only thing wonderful about it was that it was "wonderfully ugly". He was always convinced that the Great Exhibition finally killed traditional design and crafts in England.

But thirty years later Morris's ideas of decorative beauty and fitness had so altered even official taste that he was commissioned to redecorate St. James's Palace, including silk damask hangings specially designed for the Throne Room and the Reception Rooms, the painting of rich designs on the ceilings and cornices, and the making of a special paper for the hanging of the main staircase.

Little could that handful of artists and very un-business men who started the Morris firm have dreamed that they would come to such official honours as that. In fact, most of them would have been distinctly shocked at the idea. But this important work at St. James's Palace set the official seal of approval on Morris as a decorator, and the road was clear before him to honours and wealth. But he did not choose to take that road.

Nevertheless, he cared for the work he was doing, knew it to be good work, and was no more to be turned aside from it by official approval than he would have been by official disapproval. A stout common sense under all vagaries was one of Morris's qualities.

It was obvious that the firm, expanding in so many directions, needed and must have, larger premises. Converted stables were not sufficient accommodation for making carpets, and there were many other things than carpets. There was weaving, dyeing, and cotton-printing, as well as the wallpapers, and these were all trades that required space. London did not yield space, and Morris's dislike of London, which was increasing upon him as he grew older, made him desire to take his work and his work-people out of London completely, to more rural and simpler surroundings. Dyeing in particular, like paper-making and beer, required a special kind of water, and bleaching needed clean air and sun. In view of this approaching need, even before it became immediately pressing, Morris had cast a hopeful eye over some of the lovely simple Cotswold villages that lay round about Kelmscott. There were empty and unused mills that once had turned out silk yarn for Coventry ribbons. One of these villages seemed to Morris almost ideal for his needs, but there were difficulties—it was a hundred miles from London, and the stern advice of his business-manager caused it to be given up.

Then, when at last the need became really pressing, places on the outskirts of London were searched. Hemel

Hempstead and Isleworth were looked at, and West Drayton, and for a time there was thought of returning to early haunts at Crayford. Morris himself went to look at the premises there: "I saw Hall Place once more," he said, "and it made the stomach in me turn round with desire of an old house."

Finally the necessary premises were found at Merton in Surrey—that once rural spot which was the home of Nelson's heart and his last thought on the morning of Trafalgar. The premises had once been a silk-weaving factory of Huguenot refugees, and then a printing-works. The River Wandle ran by, giving water of the right quality for dyeing. In spite of these advantages Morris said that if he took these premises at Merton, "then am I for evermore a bird of this world-without-end-for-ever-lasting hole of a London".

The Merton works were only seven miles from Charing Cross, instead of the hundred Morris would have preferred.

But the Merton works had still a certain rural grace. There was a large meadow, and an orchard and vegetable garden. The banks of the Wandle and the mill-pond were set thick with willows and poplars. The neglected flower-garden by the dwelling-house was soon restored to beauty —Morris could not endure a neglected garden—and the work-sheds, weather-boarded and with red-tiled roofs, were pleasant and countrified to look upon. There was still standing a bit of medieval wall, all that remained of Merton Abbey.

There was a great deal of work and planning to be done to get the Merton works in going order. Morris fretted with impatience at all the inevitable delays and hitches, and declared he was in an agony of muddle. He was making new designs in every spare minute, for execution when the new premises were in working order. When at last this was the case a circular was issued by the firm showing all the kinds of work it was prepared to undertake.

This is the list: painted glass windows; Arras tapestry woven on the high-warp loom; carpets; embroidery; tiles; hand-made furniture; printed cotton goods; paper hangings; figured woven stuffs; furniture velvets and cloths; upholstery; general hand decoration.

How extensive and far-reaching! And all, it may be said, fundamentally sprang from Morris's brain and energy and gifts. Rossetti's description of the beginnings of the enterprise, which on the face of it seemed inevitably doomed to early decease, reads oddly in view of these solid and distinguished achievements, and the far-reaching influence of the business, not only in England, but also on the Continent. The casualness of the firm's beginnings is shown in Rossetti's words:

> A lot of us were together, and we got talking about the way in which artists did all kinds of things in olden times, designed every kind of decoration and most kinds of furniture, and some one suggested—as a lark more than anything else—that we should each put down five pounds and form a company. Fivers were blossoms of a rare growth among us in those days, and I won't swear that the table rustled with fivers. Anyhow, the firm was formed; but of course there was no deed or anything of that kind. In fact it was a mere playing at business, and Topsy was elected manager, not because we ever dreamed that he would turn out a man of business, but because he was the only one among us who had both time and money to spare. We had no idea whatever of commerical success, but it has succeeded almost in our own despite. Top's very eccentricities and independent attitude towards his patrons seem to have drawn patrons round him.

Rossetti omitted to mention that it was more than "Top's" eccentricities which attracted the patrons, but the fact that he was a designer of genius, that he had a marvellous eye for colour, that the goods he supplied were not only beautiful and of high quality but completely unlike what could be found in an England sunk in domestic ugliness.

25

With the Merton Abbey works in his possession Morris had room to stretch his mind and his plans. The setting was really singularly fortunate—so near to London, yet with the peace of the past still upon it—the sort of atmosphere in which a man who was really a medieval craftsman could work through unfretted days. A colleague of Morris's, Lewis Day, describes it:

> Imagine by the Wandle's side, an old walled garden. On the banks long, low-roofed worksheds, and a water-wheel revolving at its ease; long strips of printed cotton a-rinsing in the stream; great hanks of yarn, fresh from the indigo vat, hang drying in the air; dyers and printers moving quietly about— in all, a sunlit picture of most peaceful work.

For the Merton Abbey workshops Morris designed a series of superb patterns—his working drawings have something of the grace and vigour of nature herself, and also something of the enchanting formality he had imbibed as a boy from the study of Gerarde's Tudor *Herbal*.
On this subject of design he said himself:

> Beauty mingled with invention, founded on observation of nature, is the mainspring of decorative design. If it is not beautiful it has no right to exist; if it is not invention it becomes wearisome; if it is not founded on observation of nature it can hardly be beautiful or inventive. It is apt to become merely strange and monstrous when it departs far from nature.

His views were as clear as his patterns.
Lewis Day, in his monograph on Morris, said:

> We need not mourn the narrowness of Morris. There is strength in concentration: and the intensity of his conviction was at the root of his success. He himself believed in narrowness, and had some scorn for anyone whose love of art was more diffuse than his. He used to say, he had rather a man did not appreciate many and various forms of art, suspecting him

probably, if he did, of not loving any one of them truly. Catholicity was obnoxious to his temperament. He was not by nature critically inclined, if we assume criticism to imply weighing and soberly judging. What he did not like he disliked; that was all, and there was an end of it. Once when we were acting as judges together, I suggested that our personal feelings ought not to count for too much, and said that our disliking a thing did not make it bad. "Oh, don't it though," he answered; "what we don't like *is* bad."

He was very stubborn, and he liked to worry out for himself all the ways and methods of doing things. Instead of going to the people who were already doing a particular thing, he would tackle the problem on his own and arrive at the best way of doing it by a method of trial and error. He would "worry it out always for himself". It might not be the quickest way of arriving at results, but it suited his pugnacious temperament—he liked getting to grips with things. He made an exception to this rule in the case of dyeing, which he took great trouble to learn from the people who best practised it.

He was fundamental in his attitude towards all the crafts, as is shown in his saying about stained glass that it was essential "that the lights we stain should not be changed to dirt or ugliness". How many modern churches, or old churches with modern glass, would be truly "enlightened" had this rule been followed. The figures in the Morris firm's stained glass were designed by Burne-Jones, but the colouring of the glass was Morris's work—rather an odd arrangement, but the beautiful results show how well these two could work together. And Morris had the unfaltering colour sense which is so greatly needed when light does not simply play upon colour, but through it.

In the early days of the business, when his ideas on some matters had not then crystallized, Morris had been willing to put new glass into old churches—he did this in the Latin Chapel at Christ Church, Oxford, and at Salisbury Cathedral. But when he was working for the Society for the Protection of Ancient Buildings he found it necessary to reconsider the whole question, and his artistic conscience made him refuse any more work of that kind. For a new church he would make new glass, but not for an old one, save in the rarest and most exceptional circumstances. In the case of old churches or other buildings which "can be considered as monuments of Ancient Art", said Morris, they could not undertake the work, "as our doing so would seem to sanction the disastrous practice of so-called Restoration".

On those grounds when Dean Stanley asked him to make a window for Westminster Abbey, Morris refused. This stand made for artistic honesty by Morris did some considerable damage to the firm, as may be imagined. Valuable commissions were lost, and for long enough it was believed that they had given up stained-glass work. But it would never have occurred to Morris to yield honestly held opinions for cash. One exception he made—and this was for very personal and intimate reasons—when he put his own rich and lovely windows in the chancel of the little ancient church at Rottingdean. But those new windows did not replace old and beautiful glass, and there was no old stone tracery to run the risk of injury—one of the most serious matters in replacing old by modern glass— as the windows are plain lancets.

It is a long way from coloured church windows to a simple cottage chair, but Morris did them both. The firm's "Sussex" rush-seated chair—modelled on an old village chair—is one of the most useful and satisfactory things they ever produced. It was sold for a few shillings, and has spread everywhere.

The Morris chintzes produced at Merton have always been among the most popular of his productions—partly because of their very reasonable cost, and because a small length could be bought to cover a cushion or a chair. The purchase of a "Hammersmith" carpet, or the papering of a room in the "Pomegranate" wallpaper, was a serious

6*

financial matter, but the thinnest purse could run to a few yards of chintz. Morris, of course, designed the chintzes principally as wall-hangings—he hung his own rooms at Kelmscott Manor and Kelmscott House with them. But this was the one use the British public would not make of them. "People dressed themselves in his wall-hangings," said Mackail, "covered books with them, did this or that with them according to their fancy; but hang walls with them they would not."

Of course Morris's idea for his chintzes was that they should be hung in loose folds on the walls, like tapestry—not pasted like paper.

To read Mackail's account of the Merton Abbey works is almost like reading one of Morris's own remote romances.

"But indeed even to the present day", he says, and that "to-day" was fifty years ago,

as one turns out of the dusty high road and passes through the manager's little house, the world seems left in a moment behind. The old-fashioned garden is gay with irises and daffodils in spring, with hollyhocks and sunflowers in autumn, and full, summer by summer, of the fragrant flowering shrubs that make a London suburb into a brief June paradise. It rambles away towards the millpond with its fringe of tall poplars; the cottons lie bleaching on the grass thickly set with buttercups; the low long buildings with the clear rushing little stream running between them, and the wooden outside staircases leading to their upper story, have nothing about them to suggest the modern factory; even upon the great sunk dye-vats the sun flickers through leaves, and trout leap outside the windows of the long cheerful room where the carpet-looms are built. "To Merton Abbey", runs an entry in a visitor's diary on a day at the end of April 1882, when the new works had settled fairly down to their routine, "white hawthorn was out in the garden: we had tea with Mr. Morris in his room in the house, and left laden with marsh marigolds, wallflowers, lilac, and hawthorn." Of these flowers, and of others in their seasons, Morris often used to bring back bunches to London with him.

It is a most idyllic picture of a factory. And the interesting thing is that it worked—that at Merton Abbey, among the marigolds, with the trout jumping in the stream, goods were made which were sold at a satisfactory profit to a public whose improved taste Morris himself had so largely created. As to the quality of those goods, several generations can testify. The root of all this lay in Morris's own moral ideas—he was searching towards a *wholeness* in existence, not just a prettiness in living, of which he has often been ignorantly accused. He did not believe beauty could be wrapped round ugly things to hide them. It was because he did not believe this that he became a socialist— though his socialism has very little connection with what passes by that name now. It is difficult to imagine anyone less likely to submit to a totalitarian, State-run, robot existence than William Morris—the bare idea would have driven him to one of his berserk rages. Before all things he was an individual, and a fighting one at that.

The craftsman is bound to be an individualist by the nature of his being. As Morris said, it was the medieval craftsman's "pleasure and not his pain that made all things beautiful that were made, and lavished treasures of human hope and thought on everything that was made, from a cathedral to a porridge-pot". He also said, "the true secret of happiness *lies in the taking a genuine interest in all the details of daily life*".

The italics are Morris's own.

Of machinery he said:

> Why does a reasonable man use a machine? Surely to save labour. There are some things which a machine can do as well as a man's hand, *plus* a tool, can do them. He need not, for instance, grind his corn in a hand-quern; a little trickle of water, a wheel, and a few simple contrivances will do it all perfectly well, and leave him free to smoke his pipe, and think, or to carve the handle of his knife. . . . Perhaps a perfectly reasonable and fine man would stop there in his dealings with machinery.

But sixty or more years ago Morris was only faintly fore-seeing the robot machine, the full horror of which had not dawned to consciousness, though he was fully aware of "the ingenuity of man, which seems to be boundless in the direction of making himself unhappy".

What every man had a right to claim, he felt, was what he would himself claim as the basis of a proper working life:

> Money enough to keep him from fear of want or degradation for him and his; leisure enough from bread-earning work (even though it be pleasant to him) to give him time to read and think, and connect his own life with the life of the great world; work enough of the kind aforesaid, and praise of it, and encouragement enough to make him feel good friends with his fellows; and lastly (not least, for 'tis verily part of the bargain) his own due share of art, the chief part of which will be a dwelling that does not lack the beauty which Nature would freely allow it, if our own perversity did not turn Nature out of doors.

On the prevalent and opposing conditions to those set forth, he said: "If I were to work ten hours a day at work I despised and hated, I should spend my leisure, I hope, in political agitation, but I fear in drinking."

26

The time was now coming when Morris was to give up his leisure (a thing he valued so intensely, as it was really an opportunity for doing a different kind of work) to "political agitation" for the cause of that working man whom he had the imagination to see as himself. He knew quite well that this unpopular championship and pre-occupation would cut him off in many ways from his own circle. His wife did not like it. Burne-Jones was smitten into a pained and horrified silence. "I feel a lonely kind of a chap", said Morris at this time, in one of his few pronouncements about his own feelings.

It is believed that there were two subjects on which these close friends could never bring themselves to speak to each other—Ned on Topsy's socialism, and Topsy on Ned's accepting his baronetcy.

Morris was so occupied with his developing political ideas that there is little to record of his outer life. He said he was dwelling "somewhat low down in the valley of humiliation", and called himself "a kind of radical cobbler".

It is not necessary to go into detail about socialism as Morris saw and practised it. The name has been used to cover many shades of doctrine, and what is called socialism in one generation is nothing of the sort in the next.

In an article in the *Quarterly Review* written after his death by W. R. Lethaby and Robert Steele, they said:

> Morris was a socialist because he rebelled against the capitalist system, which imposes uniformity on craftsmanship and treats the workman as a mere unit, and against uncontrolled competition, which sacrifices beauty to cheapness, solid work to seductive shams, and art to machinery. There was, in fact, nothing modern or scientific about Morris's socialism. He turned to the Middle Ages, because what he detested did not then exist, but he never formulated a scientific scheme of socialism. Indeed, it is doubtful if he can be called a socialist at all: he objected as vigorously to the tyranny of collectivism as to that of capital. We are inclined to hazard the paradox that, if Morris was a socialist, he was so just because he was so intense an individualist.

Morris became a socialist much more because of his heart than because of his head. He admitted that his attempts to read Karl Marx he found very heavy going. After a short time he found, in spite of his most anxious desire to do so, that he could not march in step with the socialists of his day. It was not surprising, for he and they were marching to different tunes. His own thinking on the matter is obviously muddled; he is moved both by anger and by pity, and his convictions are pulled out of shape first in one way, then in another. He was a master of pattern: he wanted to make social life into a fine, graceful, and inspiring pattern—and he found he could not do it. This baffled him—for colour he had mud; for form, chaos. Added to this he had to grapple with anger, jealousy, greed, and misunderstanding.

The world of Hammersmith and Walham Green was a very different one to that he was to figure forth in his *Roots of the Mountains*:

> Thus then lived this folk in much plenty and ease of life, though not delicately or desiring things out of measure. They wrought with their hands, and wearied themselves; and they rested from their toil and were merry: to-morrow was not a burden to them, nor yesterday a thing which they would fain forget: life shamed them not, nor did death make them afraid.

Faced with the ugly reality instead of his dream, there is something rather pathetically childish about this burly, honest, well-intentioned man—indeed, more than well-intentioned, for he had the touch of greatness that comes from the willingness to sacrifice the things he cared for, the work he loved, in order to do things distasteful and utterly against the grain. The only personal satisfaction his socialist work can have given him is that it gave scope to his fighting instincts, his pugnacity. But by temperament, as well as training, he was really a long way from the people for whom he fought. He just could not understand that beer and betting meant to them what art meant to him. "The cause of art", he said in a lecture of 1884,

> is the cause of the people. We well-to-do people, those of us who live art, not as a toy, but as a thing necessary to the life of man, have for our best work the raising of the standard of life among the people. How can we of the middle class, we the capitalists and our hangers-on, help? By renouncing our class, and on all occasions when antagonism rises up between

the classes, casting in our lot with the victims; those who are condemned at the best to lack of education, refinement, leisure, pleasure, and renown; and at the worst, to a life lower than that of the most brutal of savages. There is no other way.

A statement of that sort is not going to have much influence either on the bloated capitalist, or the Northumbrian miner and the Billingsgate fish-porter.

But in Morris's own case this talk of renouncing one's class for a cause was not just an idle gesture, a flourish of rhetoric. He was a famous and admired poet, he had been elected an Honorary Fellow of his college at Oxford, he had won for himself a prosperous position as a designer and maker of beautiful things. When he became a member of the Democratic Federation he almost ceased, in the eyes of his world, to be a respectable member of society. Rebel though Morris was, and always had been in many ways, to do this, to step right outside his own world, required considerable courage. But there was nothing half-hearted about his adherence to the federation. "I am truly glad", he said, "that I have joined the only society I could find which is definitely socialistic."

In support of socialist ideas he sold the larger part of his library, the fruit of years of collecting—any lover of books will realize what that meant. Contrary to the general idea Morris was not a rich man—he did not care about money, he did not concentrate upon making it. To him the only value of money was that it could buy or produce beautiful things. The modern idea of it as a source of power never entered his unusurious head. Little would he grieve, he once said, if business failure obliged him to draw in his horns, "and live thereafter small and certain if possible". But a Morris who could not afford to buy a sheet of superfine vellum or a fourteenth-century missal, would have been a saddened and a crippled man.

He tried faithfully to plough through all the socialist gospels, but he secretly hated them. Much nearer to his mind was St. Thomas More's *Utopia*, which he read about this time—he expresses in one of his letters his surprise and gratification at More's forthcoming canonization—and *Erewhon*.

A great number of Morris's personal friends were shocked by his joining the Democratic Federation, and many of the most judicious felt it was a tragic waste of his unique powers. He gave so much of his time and energy to socialist work that his business was definitely neglected, and had it not been for the ability of his three managers the firm might have fallen into serious difficulties. More than this, the flow of Morris's designs was greatly abated, and he ceased entirely to do any creative literary work, either in verse or prose. It will be seen that when he gave himself to the Democratic Federation he did not hold much back.

A private misery perhaps helped to make this sacrifice more complete. It has been said earlier that there was something slightly strange in Morris's human contacts—he did not "give" himself to people as he did to causes and to nature and to things of beauty. But there was one exception, one weak spot in this unconscious armour—and that was his elder daughter Jenny. This adored girl, before she reached the age of twenty-one, became a partial invalid, subject to epileptic attacks. This became a nightmare to her father, partly broke down his own health, and released in him the half-concealed melancholy which was as much his natural heritage as his creative gifts. The "outwardness" of the socialist fight, and all its claims and quarrels, was in many ways a medicine to his soul.

What Morris meant by being a socialist he tells very clearly and plainly in these words:

> . . . what I mean by socialism is a condition of society in which there should be neither rich nor poor, neither master nor master's man, neither idle nor overworked, neither brainsick brain workers, nor heartsick hand workers, in a word, in which all men would be living in equality of condition, and would manage their affairs unmasterfully, and with the full

consciousness that harm to one would mean harm to all—the realization at last of the meaning of the word *Commonweatlh*.

Now this view of socialism which I hold to-day, and hope to die holding, is what I began with . . . in my position of a well-to-do man, not suffering from the disabilities which oppress a working man at every step, I feel that I might never have been drawn into the practical side of the question if an ideal had not forced me to seek towards it. . . . Apart from the desire to produce beautiful things, the leading passion of my life has been and is hatred of modern civilization . . . its mastery and its waste of mechanical power, its commonwealth so poor, its enemies of the commonwealth so rich, its stupendous organization—for the misery of life! Its contempt of simple pleasures which everyone could enjoy but for its folly. Its eyeless vulgarity which has destroyed art, the one certain solace of labour. All this I felt then as now, but I did not know why it was so. The hope of the past time was gone, the struggles of mankind for many ages had produced nothing but this sordid, aimless, ugly confusion; the immediate future seemed to me likely to intensify all the present evils by sweeping away the last survivals of the days before the present dull squalor of civilization had settled down on the world. This was a bad look-out indeed, and, if I may mention myself as a personality and not as a mere type, especially so to a man of my disposition, careless of metaphysics and religion, as well as of scientific analysis, but with a deep love of the earth and the life on it, and passion for the history of the past of mankind. Think of it! Was it all to end in a counting-house on the top of a cinder-heap, with Podsnap's drawing-room in the offing, and a whig committee dealing out champagne to the rich and margarine to the poor in such convenient proportions as would make all men contented together, though the pleasure of the eyes was gone from the world, and the place of Homer was to be taken by Huxley? Yes, believe me, in my heart, when I really forced myself to look toward the future, that is what I saw in it, and, as far as I could tell, scarce anyone seemed to think it worth while to struggle against such a consummation of civilization. So there I was in a fine pessimistic end of life, if it had not somehow dawned on me that amidst all this filth of civilization the seeds of a great change, what we and others call social revolutions were beginning to germinate. The whole face of things was changed to me by that discovery, and all I had to do then in order to become a socialist was to hook myself on to the practical movement, which, as before said, I have tried to do as well as I could . . . the consciousness of revolution stirring amidst me, luckier than many others of artistic perceptions, from crystallizing into a mere railer against "progress" on the one hand, and on the other from wasting time and energy in any of the numerous schemes by which the quasi-artistic of the middle classes hope to make art grow when it has no longer any root, and thus I became a practical socialist.

It is heavy going. Morris, who could inlay his words like enamel in poetry, was a poor speaker, debater, or explainer of his political beliefs. His sentences are too long, pointless and vague, they wander without always getting anywhere. The effect he had on a socialist platform was more due to his honest personality, his complete absence of sham, than to his words. Yet it is plain from that extract from his account of "How I Became a Socialist" that Morris was a natural fighter. In his very early socialist days he was as happy and as convinced of his mission as any Knight of the Round Table who had been given a particularly fearsome dragon to slay—the only trouble was that the British working man was not very good in the part of the rescued damsel.

There was nothing roundabout in Morris. His convictions were direct, not abstract and academic, as can be seen in two more statements of his.

. . . in looking into matters social and political I have but one rule, that in thinking of the condition of any body of men I should ask myself, "How could you bear it yourself? What would you feel if you were poor against the system under which you live?" I have always been uneasy when I had to ask myself that question, and of late years I have had to ask it so often, that I have seldom had it out of my mind.

And the following passage.

I can see no use in people having political freedom unless they use it as an instrument for leading reasonable and manlike lives; no good even in education if, when they are educated, people have only slavish work to do, and have to live lives too much beset with sordid anxiety for them to be able to think and feel with the more fortunate people who produced art and poetry and great thoughts.

How deeply convinced Morris was is most plainly shown in the terrible "Chants for Socialists", which he wrote in those years. That a poet who had written *Sigurd the Volsung* and the *Earthly Paradise* could turn out such clumsy stuff shows how conviction can eclipse taste—it is the more remarkable in the case of Morris, for in every other way he was an artist in all he did.

It is easy to understand how the spectacle of Morris writing such halting verse and preaching at street corners in the slums must have affected his friends. It made them feel extremely uncomfortable, as the spectacle of a man actually practising what he believes usually does. They wanted to look the other way. They felt, above all, that it was such a waste of his peculiar powers. As his friend Lewis Day said:

The sight of such a man spending his great gifts and wondrous energies in holding forth to a dozen or so of "comrades'" leagues away from any right understanding of him, was grotesque enough almost to make one doubt his sense of humour . . . Nevertheless the least sympathetic of his audience could hardly see him on the platform and not be impressed by his wonderful personality; he looked the man he was, powerfully built, thick-set, stalwart and sturdy, without any swagger, but with the air of a conqueror as he stood up to speak; an open face of fresh complexion, unshaven and rather ragged beard; his hair, grizzled and curly, that gave him the look of a lion; good grey eyes that could twinkle with merriment, light up with enthusiasm, or flush with indignation; a voice that deepened as he spoke; action and speech so sudden, it seemed it must be spontaneous.

Most of Morris's friends were divided between annoyance and pity at his becoming an active socialist. Few seemed to have realized the innate nobility which drove him into that path—a path which grew more and more distasteful to all his instincts the longer he walked upon it. If he had ever been innocent enough to believe that socialists, just because they were socialists, were solely concerned with the welfare of mankind, it did not take him very long, idealist though he always was at heart, to realize that socialists would quarrel and do each other down, just like other human beings.

27

It is needless, and it would be very dull, to go into all the squabbles of the different socialist organizations of those years in the last quarter of the nineteenth century. It is only as they concern William Morris that they have any interest here. He himself after a time found it only too easy to quarrel with the Socialist Democratic Federation, with which he had first allied himself, and as a consequence he and some like-minded fellows formed the Socialist League. To this league Morris (as he had been to the young men at Oxford in earlier years) was a rock of defence, not to speak of the banner on the top of it. He supplied money for the cause, a thing he had done so easily and unconsciously all his life that everybody took it as one of the laws of nature. He started a monthly magazine called *The Commonwealth*, which later became a weekly. It was for this publication he wrote that lovely thing *A Dream of John Ball*, and also *News From Nowhere*. English literature owes a real debt to socialism if it caused the writing of these two prose romances. They are permanent and full of beauty, and at the time they were written they were entirely new.

From such scenes as they set forth of a past England and

an imagined future England, there is an air of bathos in
going to an English police-court, but that is where Morris
was landed for the first time in his life. It is a silly little
tale, but characteristic of the happenings of that time.

At one of the open-air meetings of the Socialist League
at Limehouse there was a collision with the police, who
arrested eight of the socialists who had not been doing
anything in particular, and they were accused of obstruct-
ing a public thoroughfare and resisting the police in the
execution of their duty. Morris, of course, was present at
the Thames Police Court next morning when the eight
prisoners were brought to trial. The magistrate, a Mr.
Saunders, sentenced one of the prisoners to two months'
hard labour and imposed fines on the other seven. This
was greeted by cries of "Shame!" from Morris and others,
and there was some hustling and pushing. Morris was
there and then accused of "disorderly conduct", and of
striking a policeman, which he flatly denied. Whereupon,
this odd conversation took place:

Magistrate: What are you?
Morris: I am an artist and literary man, pretty well known,
I think, throughout Europe.
Magistrate: I suppose you did not intend to do this?
Morris: I never struck him at all.
Magistrate: Well, I will let you go.
Morris: But I have not done anything.
Magistrate: Well, you can stay if you like.
Morris: I don't want to stay.

A curious little scene in the dingy police-court, but a bit
of Morris's history. That he voluntarily suffered such things
is sufficient proof of the reality of his convictions. Ugliness
does not greatly disturb many people. They do not notice
it, or even if they do, think it does not much matter. To
Morris ugliness of living was a symptom of a deep-rooted
disease. He expressed the effect it had on him when he
said the following:

On Sunday I went a-preaching Stepney way. My visit intensely depressed me, as these eastern visits always do: the mere stretch of houses, the mass of utter shabbiness and uneventfulness, sits upon me like a nightmare.

Morris gave his money freely to the socialist cause; it was, however, a far greater sacrifice to him to give his Sundays— always a specially depressing day in London, even in the better parts of it—to Stepney and the Mile End Road and Limehouse, instead of the gentle beauty of Kelmscott.

One in particular of these dreary London Sundays was to become famous in the socialist annals. It was known as "Bloody Sunday", because the police in great force and two squadrons of the Life Guards were used to quell an intended demonstration of the unemployed in Trafalgar Square. Serious rioting and probable bloodshed was feared on this Sunday, 13 November 1887. But the forces of authority were so well handled, and those of the unemployed and the socialists so badly—Morris was marching among them— that the whole thing ended in a humiliating collapse. Of bloodshed there was actually very little, in spite of the name given to the day. One young man, Alfred Linnell, died in hospital as the result of injuries received in the struggle with the police. Morris had written indignantly on another occasion:

I may note here for the benefit of well-to-do West-enders that the police are incredibly rough and brutal to the poor people in the East End.

The whole affair sickened Morris of both sides—the brutality of those in authority, and the feebleness, and, as he felt, cowardice of those in revolt. For the young man who died so ineffectually for the cause, he felt a harrowed pity. Alfred Linnell was given a public funeral. In pouring December rain a great procession marched from Soho to Bow Cemetery, where the funeral service was read in the winter dark by the light of a lantern.

"The scene at the grave", wrote Morris a few days later,

was the strangest sight I have ever seen, I think. It was most impressive to witness; there was to me something awful (I can use no other word) in such a tremendous mass of people, unorganized, unhelped, and so harmless and good-tempered.

Morris spoke at the graveside on that "drear-nighted December", very simple words:

Our friend who lies here has had a hard life, and met with a hard death; and if society had been differently constructed his life might have been a delightful, a beautiful, and a happy one. It is our business to begin to organize for the purpose of seeing that such things shall not happen; to try to make this earth a beautiful and happy place.

The voice of Morris himself is rather like that of a child crying in the dark.

28

Morris did not lose his life in the cause of socialism (though in the days when he had faith in it he would not have shrunk from that sacrifice if necessary), but to a large extent he lost his health in that service. He was in the middle fifties, he had twice suffered attacks of rheumatic fever, and he was of a gouty tendency. To such a man, standing preaching at street corners in bleak north-east winds or in rain, lecturing in cold or stuffy (often, as he said, dirty and smelly) little halls and rooms, travelling considerable distances in and round London, and far afield to places so unpleasing to him as Leeds, Bradford, Blackburn, and Glasgow, did very definite harm to his health. These toils brought on a serious attack of gout, from which he never quite recovered, and it is rather pathetic to find him, in the midst of the pangs of gout, definitely rejoicing that he is, for a time, at liberty to lie in his own house and let the sun slide across his couch, while he amuses himself with "rubbishy novels".

Another thing he had given up entirely for over three years was the work, so natural and delightful to him, of creative writing. But after this long absence from felicity he began to slip back into his native element, first by way of translating the *Odyssey* of Homer. This large task, to the horror, of course, of all proper and cloistered scholars, Morris did in the intervals of rushing about to socialist meetings and attending to the needs of his business, even such absurd sidelines of the business as visiting a lady in Hans Place who said she wanted his advice on decorative work, which sounded like a profitable order for the firm, but when a rather irritated Morris arrived at her house it was to find that she wanted his opinion of her poker-work! No doubt she got it.

It is not surprising, amid all these activities, that Morris declared his time was "a mere heap of chopped straw". Nevertheless, with these broken bits of leisure it was his instinct to do something that would make a bit more pattern in his life. So he chose as his recreation and escape the work of translating the *Odyssey*. Having this task in hand to fall back upon was evidently a refreshment to him, as a woman may take up her embroidery frame for release from everyday cares. When it was completed he had the somewhat lost feeling most writers know when a book is finished. It was published in two volumes, one in the spring and the other in the autumn of 1887.

Morris's translation is a very faithful one, and beautiful and agreeable to read. But, says Mackail, it has not taken its place as the standard English translation of the *Odyssey*, probably because there is not one. The general public is not particularly avid of translations of Homer, and scholars do not need translations; so in a sense Morris's work fell between two stools, except in so far as he gained his own honest craftsman's joy in doing the job. Morris's idea of a holiday was always a change of occupation—not doing nothing.

At any rate his adopted Hammersmith gave him credit

for being something in the literary line. He tells how on
one occasion some of the local toughs meeting him, yelled
out: "Shakespeare, yah!" But this tribute he put down to
the fact that he was wearing a grey cloak, in which "people
doubt whether I be a brigand or a parson". He also records
that a small boy, swinging uncomfortably on one of the
iron gates in Rivercourt Road, called out to him: "Have
a ride, Morris"; while the driver of a greengrocer's cart
near high-walled Nazareth House in the same region,
called out: "Socialist!" as he went by. "I don't think",
said Morris modestly, "this was meant to be compli-
mentary." But he admitted he was a little upset because
a socialist outing in which he was involved was taken for a
"detachment of the Salvation Army". On another occasion
he said the socialists were becoming so quarrelsome among
themselves that he thought he would have to join the
Quakers.

More even than by the socialist quarrels was he per-
turbed by "the frightful ignorance and want of impressi-
bility of the average English workman", which, he said,
"floors me at times".

And not only ignorance, but complete absence. His
delightful lecture on "Feudal England" was actually delivered by him to an audience of nine people. Yet in that
lecture there were many things that matter to the working
man; the very reasons of his condition, as he can learn
them from history. It should have been worth his while
to step across the road, if for nothing more than to hear
Morris re-tell the tale of the death of bad King John from
and ancient folk-story, which, he said:

> I can here make bold to quote from memory, without depart-
> ing very widely from the old text, since the quaint wording of
> the original, and the spirit of bold and blunt heroism which it
> breathes, have fixed it in my mind for ever.
> The king, you must remember, had halted at Swinestead
> Abbey, in Lincolnshire, in his retreat from the hostile barons
> and their French allies, and had lost all his baggage by the

surprise of the advancing tide in the Wash; so that he might well be in a somewhat sour mood.

Says the tale: So the king went to meal in the hall, and before him was a loaf, and he looked grimly on it and said: "For how much is such a loaf sold in this realm?"

"Sir, for one penny," said they.

Then the king smote the board with his fist and said: "By God, if I live for one year such a loaf shall be sold for twelve pence!"

That heard one of the monks who stood thereby, and he thought and considered that his hour and time to die was come, and that it would be a good deed to slay so cruel a king and so evil a lord.

So he went into the garden and plucked plums and took out of them the stones, and did venom in them each one; and he came before the king and sat on his knee, and said:

"Sir, by St. Austin, this fruit is of our garden."

Then the king looked evilly on him and said, "Assay them, monk!"

So the monk took and ate thereof, nor changed countenance any whit: and the king ate thereafter.

But presently afterwards the monk swelled and turned blue, and fell down and died before the king: then waxed the king sick at heart, and he also swelled and died, and so he ended his days.

But only nine people came to listen to that marvellous tale, and all the pictures of history that went before and after it, and then Morris's conclusion and summing up:

The workman of to-day, if he could realize the position of his forerunner, has some reason to envy him: the feudal serf worked hard, and lived poorly, and produced a rough livelihood for his master; whereas the modern workman, working harder still, and living little if any better than the serf, produces for his master a state of luxury of which the old lord of the manor never dreamed. The workman's powers of production are multiplied a thousandfold; his own livelihood remains pretty much where it was. The balance goes to his master and the crowd of useless, draggle-tailed knaves and fools who pander

to his idiotic sham desires, and who, under the pretentious title
of the intellectual part of the middle classes, have in their turn
taken the place of the medieval jester.

Most of Morris's friends disliked and distrusted the whole
socialist doctrine, and would by no means follow him on
that adventure, but there was one friend of his early days
who stuck to him through everything from youth to age,
and that was Charles Faulkner. In the Oxford days he
was with Morris as a member of the "brotherhood"; then
he was with him as a member of the firm; then, finally, he
was a member of the Socialist League. This steady, con-
sistent, faithful friendship was one of the inner props of
Topsy's life.

Morris was not of an introspective nature; he was always
going forward so eagerly that he had neither time nor
much inclination for looking backwards and inwards. But
it is not unnatural to assume that his John Ball is expressing
a good deal of his own feeling about the years of socialist
struggles in which he was involved when he says:

> Men fight and lose the battle, and the thing that they fought
> for comes about in spite of their defeat, and when it comes
> turns out not to be what they meant.

29

One beautiful and permanent thing, at least, came out
of Morris's socialist convictions, and that was his prose
tale, *A Dream of John Ball*. It stands apart from all his
other work in prose or in verse, and had he written nothing
else and done nothing else, would ensure that his name
should be remembered. All of Morris is in it—the little
boy who stood at gaze in Canterbury Cathedral, the
romantic and crusading undergraduate, the craftsman, the
artist, the poet, the historian, the "Comrade Morris" who

stood at the graveside of an unknown young man killed in the riots of "Bloody Sunday", the Englishman who loved his country with a depth and poignancy little guessed by those who would more cheaply call themselves patriots.

A Dream of John Ball was the direct fruit of Morris's socialism, as it was written for and first appeared as a serial in *The Commonwealth*. Had he not been a socialist he would probably never have written it. This book was the first of a series of prose romances, which from that time onwards to his death were to be Morris's chief form of literary work. But the *Dream* is in a category by itself, and except that it is written in prose, as are they, must not be associated with *The Roots of the Mountains* and *The House of the Wolfings*, semi-historical though they are; still less with those far away romances like *The Well at the World's End*, *The Glittering Plain*, and *The Sundering Flood*, which are grown-up fairy-tales for such people as have kept, as Morris did, their hearts young enough to love them.

John Ball is a work alone and perfect, and because of this must have a little space and quotation given to it.

The book opens very simply with Morris telling in his own person of the sort of "architectural dreams" he often had.

"This dream", he writes,

is as it were a present of an architectural peep-show. I see some beautiful and noble building new made, as it were, for the occasion, as clearly as if I were awake . . . Some Elizabethan house with its scrap of earlier fourteenth-century building . . . Or sometimes 'tis a splendid collegiate church, untouched by restoring parson or architect, standing amid an island of shapely trees and flower-beset cottages of thatched grey stone and cob, amidst the narrow stretch of bright green water-meadows that wind between the sweeping Wiltshire downs, so well beloved of William Cobbett. Or some new-seen and yet familiar cluster of houses in a grey village of the Upper Thames overtopped by the delicate tracery of a fourteenth-century church; or even sometimes the very buildings of the past untouched by the degradation of the sordid utilitarianism that cares not and knows not of beauty and history: as once, when I was journeying (in a dream of the night) down the well-remembered reaches of the Thames betwixt Streatley and Wallingford, where the foot-hills of the White Horse fall back from the broad stream, I came upon a clear-seen medieval town, standing up with roof and tower and spire within its walls, grey and ancient, but untouched from the days of its builders of old.

Then he goes on to tell how he awoke (as he thought) to "find myself lying on a strip of wayside waste by an oak copse just outside a country village". In this *Dream* he had awoken in the fourteenth century in a Kentish village. It was a beautiful village; the church windows were so newly carved that the dust of the stonecutter's chisel still lay on the midsummer grass below them, and in the pot-house parlour the Dreamer was enchanted by its stout oaken table that "went up and down the room", with a carved oak chair by the open chimney-corner, and the plaster above the panelling "wrought in a pattern of rose-stems".

Then he comes upon John Ball, the "hedge-priest", preaching to the people who stand silently under the sky to hear him, and listens to all his words and his memories, including the memory of when he was immured in prison so short a time before.

"For hearken, my friends and helpers," said John Ball to the villagers who stood around him,

many days ago, when April was yet young, I lay there, and the heart that I had strung up to bear all things because of the fellowship of men and the blessed saints and the angels and those that are, and those that are to be, this heart, that I had strung up like a strong bow, fell into feebleness, so that I lay there a-longing for the green fields and the whitethorn bushes and the lark singing over the corn, and the talk of good fellows round the ale-house bench, and the babble of the little children, and the team on the road and the beasts a-field, and all the life of earth; and I alone all the while, near my foes and afar from my friends, mocked and flouted and starved with cold and hunger; and so weak was my heart that though I longed for all these things yet I saw them not, nor knew them but as names; and I longed so sore to be gone that I chided myself that I had once done well: and I said to myself:

"Forsooth, hadst thou left thy tongue between thy teeth thou mightest have been something, if it had been but a parson of a town, and comfortable to many a poor man; and then mightest thou have clad here and there the naked back, and filled the empty belly, and helpen many, and men would have spoken well of thee, and of thyself thou hadst thought well; and all this hast thou lost for lack of a word here and there to some great man, and a little winking of the eyes amidst murder and wrong and untruth; and now thou art nought and helpless, and the hemp for thee is sown and grown and heckled and spun, and lo there, the rope for thy gallows-tree!—all for nought, for nought."

Forsooth, my friends, thus I thought and sorrowed in my feebleness that I had not been a traitor to the Fellowship of the Church, for e'en so evil was my foolish imagination. . . . So I became a man once more, and I rose up to my feet and went up and down my prison what I could for my hopples, and into my mouth came words of good cheer, even such as we to-day have sung, and stoutly I sang them, even as we now have sung them; and then did I rest me, and once more thought of those pleasant fields where I would be, and all the life of man and beast about them, and I said to myself that I shall see them once more before I died, if but once more.

Then John Ball finished his preaching to the villagers with the words:

Ye shall not lack for the fields ye have tilled, nor the houses ye have built, nor the cloth ye have woven, all these shall be yours, and whatever ye will of all the earth beareth; then shall no man mow the deep grass for another, while his own kine lack cow-meat; and he that soweth shall reap, and the reaper shall eat in fellowship the harvest that in fellowship he hath won; and he that buildeth a house shall dwell in it with those that he biddeth of his free will; and the tithe barns shall garner the wheat for all men to eat of when the seasons are untoward, and the rain-drift hideth the sheaves in August; and all shall be without money and without price. Faithfully and merrily then shall all men keep the holidays of the Church in peace of body and joy of heart. And man shall help man, and the saints in heaven shall be glad, because men no more fear each other; and the Church shall be ashamed, and shall hide his churlishness till it be gone, and he be no more a churl; and fellowship shall be established in heaven and on the earth.

And the dreamer of this *Dream*, who is Morris, sees how men in those days lived and fought and were willing to die for the freedom they desired, and "against villeinage which is waning", and "against usury which is waxing". He holds that strange vigil in the village church with John Ball, and sets down their talk there—John Ball with a man not to be born for many centuries, William Morris with a man dead as many centuries: "Betwixt the Living and the Dead."

After the intensity with which this *Dream* brings alive that far past, makes it live before our eyes, so that it is both felt and visualized, even to the way the moonlight fell upon the grass in that departed century, we can feel in our own bones the kind of shock with which Morris came awake in the Hammersmith of his own day, "lying in my familiar bed, the south-westerly gale rattling the venetian blinds and making their holdfasts squeak".

"I got up presently", he ends his book,

and going to the window looked out on the winter morning; the river was before me broad between outer bank and bank, but it was nearly dead ebb, and there was a wide space of mud on each side of the hurrying stream, driven on the faster as it seemed by the push of the south-west wind. On the other side of the water the few willow-trees left us by the Thames Conservancy looked doubtfully alive against the bleak sky and the rows of wretched-looking blue-slated houses, although, by the way, the latter were the backs of a sort of street of "villas" and not a slum; the road in front of the house was sooty and muddy at once, and in the air was that sense of dirty discomfort which one is never quit of in London. The morning was harsh too, and though the wind was from the south-west it was as cold as a north wind; and yet amidst of it all, I thought of the corner of the next bight of the river which I could not quite see from where I was, but over which one can see clear of houses and into Richmond Park, looking like the open country, and harsh as was the January wind, they seemed to woo me towards the countryside, where away from the miseries of the "Great Wen" I might of my own will carry on a day-dream of the friends I had made in the dream of the night and against my will.

It was for *The Dream of John Ball* that Burne-Jones made his famous drawing of Adam and Eve and their two babies with the verse underneath:

> When Adam delved,
> And Eve span,
> Who was then the gentleman?

The whole rich and decorative design enclosed in one of Morris's characteristic borders.

The Dream and *News From Nowhere* are both of them the fair fruit of Morris's socialist convictions, *News From Nowhere* being an example of the Utopian romance to which Morris has given more charm and feeling than is usual in such works. The descriptions are enchanting, even if the people are somewhat lacking in the qualities of humanity.

30

But after many years of hard and devoted work in the socialist cause, Morris lost not his convictions but his faith —his faith, that is, in any active and worthwhile results. The petty squabbling and disagreements, the kind of nose-to-the-ground attitude sickened him. He was not a patient man by nature, but he had shown extraordinary patience in his work with his socialist colleagues, sacrificing his time (which he valued above everything), his money (which he thought little of), and his strength (which he could not replace). Then he suddenly decided to make an end of it, and go back to his own job of craftsmanship, and if he could not make a better world, to make at any rate a few things which he knew were good. Perhaps he began to think that political work was not what he was intended for—as many of his friends had been thinking for years. Certainly he longed acutely for the peace and satisfaction of making things with his hands and brain. He was no longer a young man; he was no longer a very robust man. His fine health had gone down the wind and the rain of the London streets and wastes, which in their ugliness and depression had lowered his vitality and haunted him too long. He had fought to keep a little beauty in them, as he had fought to make a more tolerable life for the workers who perforce dwelt in those miserable slums; but they were too sunk and deadened to respond, or even understand what he was talking about. The gap on both sides was too wide: Morris could not cross it.

Certain gaps were not so unbridgeable, and there is a little story to illustrate this, full of the authentic Morris flavour. It is told by Sir William Richmond in his *Recollections*, and relates to Hammersmith, where both Richmond and Morris lived not very far from each other: Richmond at Beavor Lodge, behind whose high garden walls a little bit of the old rural Hammersmith was entrapped, as it was in Morris's garden at Kelmscott House.

On the south bank of the Thames between Hammersmith and Barnes Bridge there was an avenue of willows shading the towpath. The Thames Conservancy—a body with whom Morris was continuously and on principle at war—cut down a number of these pleasant trees and sold them for twelve shillings each to a cricket-bat maker. This was done at a time when both Morris and Richmond happened to be away from Hammersmith. When they

7

returned and saw the pathetic gaps in the row of willows they were both furious, and decided to beard the Conservancy ogres in their den. Enlisting the support of a neighbour living at Hammersmith Terrace, which looks out on the Thames, the three men set out for the city, Morris telling Richmond that he was to do the talking, and Richmond urging Morris to open the attack, saying that he would back him up hard. Both still gracefully trying to slip into the background, they were ushered into the board-room, and to them entered a certain Captain Burstall, "a giant of a man who looked as if he had fed on rum all his life", said Richmond, describing the scene; and he adds with enjoyment: "Morris was nervous!" He continues with the tale:

Then with a stentorian voice the Burstall gave utterance to these memorable words:

"What the Hell do you b——y chaps want? What is your b——y business?" Wapping could not have supplied more fruity language.

All Morris's nerve returned. "We've come to ask you savage b——y chaps why the Hell you have cut down a pleasant grove of willows?" he thundered.

"What the Hell's that to you?" was the quick response.

"We mean", said Morris firmly, "to kick up the devil's own row about this b——y affair, and to demand a very Hell of reparation from the b——y Board!"

Captain Burstall had found his match in strong language. It roused his respect. He calmed down. We put the matter before him plainly. He softened visibly. Finally we got our way; he consented to order fresh trees to be planted. But it was all due to the fact that Burstall evidently liked Morris. He recognized him as a congenial spirit, and on coming out Morris likewise said, "Not a bad chap, after all, is he?" The trees were planted, and the matter dropped.

Topsy certainly came into his own on that occasion, and probably Captain Burstall took him for a retired mariner, the late master or "old man" of some phantom *Skylark*.

31

Few of Morris's friends could refrain from writing about him, which is very much to our advantage and satisfaction. His character and personality were too marked to escape notice. He was himself pleasantly unconscious of this; he just did and said what he felt like doing and saying without any thought of its effect on others. Had he known it he would have been surprised and, on the whole, annoyed that people were writing things about him in their diaries and letters and reminiscences.

William Richmond has quite a lot to say about his friend that is interesting:

> The voice, the gesture, and a mixture of waywardness and wisdom it was that proclaimed his individuality. He was funny without knowing it, wise without knowing it . . . a great big generous character, though a bit narrow from his thoughts running in a groove.

Living as they did so close together in Hammersmith, the two had many prolonged discussions together, though Morris complained occasionally that Richmond's stories were "interminable". Legend states that on a certain occasion Morris at Kelmscott House listened to one of Richmond's yarns till three o'clock and then forcibly turned him out. At six o'clock in the morning there was a ring at the bell. "That will be Willie Richmond come back to finish his story!" cried Morris.

Richmond, with an artist's eye delighted in Kelmscott Manor.

"Such a romantic place I hardly ever saw," he said:

> a stone house, stone roof under which you can perambulate among the rafters, and king posts over the whole range of the rooms. . . . Morris is quite splendid company, English to the marrow of his bones, original, energetic, and simple as a boy.

"He saw new beauties in his delightful home every day", Richmond wrote,

> He loved to study the old timbers in the roof, the stone paths of the garden, the lichen-grown stone of its walls. He loved the stone pavement of the basement, but confessed to permitting it to be hidden by Oriental rugs in the winter. For in his way he liked comfort, if it was not too far removed from what was possible in the fifteenth century or even earlier. What a treat it was to visit an old church with him! and how refreshing was his language of disgust at the vandals of architecture who "restored". He would make old buildings young again in five minutes of his brilliant talk.

Another friend of Morris who wrote illuminatingly about him was Wilfrid Scawen Blunt, and it is plain from *My Diaries* that he was not only interested in Morris, but attached to him with some warmth. Till 1889 the two men had only met occasionally, but that summer Blunt went to stay at Kelmscott Manor, and during hours of gudgeon fishing got to know Morris as he really was.

"Morris at that time", Blunt says, "was in a mood of reaction from his socialistic fervour. He had quarrelled with Hyndman. He was disgusted at the personal jealousies in the cause and at their cowardice in action."

Morris, with those who dared to argue with him boldly, Blunt goes on to say, was a delightful companion:

> He was intolerant of the conventional talk of society, and had little sympathy with ideas foreign to his own. . . . In his domestic life Morris was too busy to be unhappy, and of too sanguine a temperament to worry himself much over past disappointments; yet disappointments cannot but have been his. He had a strong and affectionate heart, and had centred his home affections on his two children, and the younger, May, had just made an engagement he disapproved, while the elder, Jenny, who had been his pride as a child for her intellectual faculties had overworked her brain and was now subject to epileptic fits. It was touching now at Kelmscott to watch Morris's solicitude for this poor girl on whom his chief home love was bestowed.

KELMSCOTT MANOR: THE OFFICE YARD.

Of Kelmscott Manor itself and the life there, Blunt says:

Kelmscott Manor was a romantic house, and the life there extremely primitive. There were few of the conveniences of modern life. The rooms below and also on the upper floor were all passage rooms opening one into another, and in order to reach the tapestried chamber in which we sat in the evenings, it was necessary to pass to and fro through Morris's own bedroom, in which he lay at night in a great square Elizabethan four-post bed, an arrangement which would have been of extreme discomfort to anyone less tolerant of such things than he and less indifferent to his personal convenience. It was the same thing in the daytime. He worked at the designs he was making for his carpets, and at his drawings and the correcting of his proofs in a room where he was liable every minute to disturbance. Such discomforts had been submitted to by our forefathers, and why not, he thought, by us. It was this insensitiveness to his surroundings that enabled him to deal with the prodigious volume of work which he daily assigned himself, both manual and intellectual.

In illustration of this "insensitiveness" (though a more suitable word might be chosen) an earlier visitor recorded how entering a room in which she found Morris working, she was about to retreat hastily when he looked up and said: "Oh, come in, I'm only writing poetry."

Blunt gives excellent glimpses of Morris on the river, sitting in a punt for hours fishing.

"In all matters concerning the river", he says,

he took a passionate and proprietary interest, cherishing a special grudge against the Thames Conservancy, a body which interfered with individual rights, and whose legitimate authority he denied. Against these he constantly inveighed. He had, too, in memory of Oxford, to engage in wordy warfare with the bargees, and had a strong vocabulary of abuse for them, which he did not spare. When on the river he affected a rough manner even with his fellows in the boat, and scorned to apologize if accidents through his fault occurred, all of which was in keeping with his appearance which was that of a Norwegian sea-captain, rather than a poet, and of this he was proud. He was very dogmatic, with violent likes and dislikes.

Blunt stayed with Morris at Kelmscott Manor, and Morris stayed with Blunt at his old and romantically secluded Sussex home, New Buildings, where woods took the place of water. Once when there Morris expressed dissatisfaction at the lovely weather, and told his host: "I am a man of the North. I am disappointed at the fine weather we are having here. I had hoped it would rain, so that I could sit indoors and watch it beating on the windows."

That was said by Morris in the spring of the last year of his life, and he was ill and fretting again for Iceland, thinking, like a child, that it would restore him to his old health and vigour.

After Morris's death Blunt wrote:

> He is the most wonderful man I have known, unique in this, that he had no thought for any thing or person, including himself, but only for the work he had in hand. . . . I have seen him tender to his daughter Jenny, and nice with May and with his wife, but I doubt if he thought of them much when he did not see them, and his life was not arranged in reference to them.

That beautiful, rather melancholy old house, New Buildings, has a further link with Morris than the fact that he stayed there with its owner. After Morris's death his widow when disposing of the furniture at Kelmscott House in Hammersmith gave the dining-room table to Wilfrid Scawen Blunt, and it is now at New Buildings. This was the dining-room table made for the Red House in all the flush of youth. It is now mellowed into a dignified solidity and colour, and becomes an historic piece of furniture. When Morris's library was sold after his death, Blunt bought his Gerarde's *Herbal*, Berner's *Froissart*, and Malory's *Morte d'Arthur* in the Copland edition of 1557.

But in spite of the links with New Buildings it is not in those lovely Sussex woods that the spirit of William Morris revisits the glimpses of the moon, but on the upper reaches of the Thames, where the water still runs softly since he ended his song.

32

The decision to abandon further active socialist work, after the dreary and unproductive years he had sacrificed on that altar, gave Morris a sense of release, though his conscience was still troubled over the matter.

"I am not in a good temper with myself", he wrote: "I cannot shake off the feeling that I might have done much more in these recent matters than I have, though I really don't know what I could have done; but I feel beaten and humbled."

But it was not in Morris's nature to sit down in a beaten mood. His remedy for any ill, material or spiritual, was work—work that employed his hand and filled his mind. Till he became a socialist he had always desired that his work, though it might be hard, a thing he did not mind, should be congenial. But the work he did in lecturing and preaching in the shabby slums of Hammersmith and Walham Green and ugly outer waste places, had been utterly uncongenial to his soul, after his first high hopes had faded. He had set off—with that "small boy" attitude which was always part of Topsy—believing that at the waving of the Red Flag the Castle of Giant Despair would fall, that poverty, misery, and dreary ugliness would disappear, and that people would learn to live happily and simply by the good work of their hands. He half fearfully and half excitedly thought there might be some sort of a revolution, with possible bloodshed, before this happened, but was convinced the result would be worth the troubled few days, which was all he appeared to anticipate.

He grew up considerably during his socialist years, and growing up made him unhappy. He also felt that his

efforts were achieving just nothing. So he decided to return
to the kind of work where he could achieve something to
his mind. He was a practical man, as well as a poet. Moreover, he had received several indications that "Brother
Ass" the body was grumbling at being overdriven. He
was not an old man, but he may have known, as people
often do know in some strange way, that his remaining
years would not be many. "I wish I was not so damned
old", he said, when he was still in the fifties.

He, who was so naturally and instinctively the medieval
craftsman, lacked completely what that craftsman possessed
as naturally as the air he breathed—faith. Morris in his
maturity had no belief in any future life. To him the
Gothic cathedrals he loved so passionately did not rear
their fretted stone to the glory of God so much as to
honour of mankind. In his mind beauty and good work-
manship were their own reward, and did not need to be
linked with an unseen world. He who was at home in a
fairy and mythical kind of existence was so perhaps because he had the sad heathen heart of the changeling. He
exaggerated the importance of beauty, because for him it
was everything. It had to give meaning to existence, for
to him there was nothing beyond this life, and death was
the end, the "Sundering Flood". Such a belief, or rather
unbelief, held honestly and sadly by this great-hearted man,
cut him off from so many things he needed. He tried to
substitute the continuity of mankind for the continuity of
existence, but it did not work. In his soul he knew that it
was the Ages of Faith which had produced the most
glorious works of man, and though the works meant so
much to him, the faith he could not hold.

He loved Chaucer all his life and called him "Master",
but he knew there was that gulf between them, and it
added poignancy to his cry, as one who stretches his hands
across a bridgeless chasm, in the Envoi to the *Earthly
Paradise*, when he bids his book seek the Land of Matters
Unforgot, saying:

Hast thou heard
That therein I believe I have a friend,
Of whom for love I may not be afeared?
It is to him indeed I bid thee wend;
Yea, he perchance may meet thee ere thou think,
Dying so far off from the hedge of bay,
Thou idle singer of an empty day!

Well, think of him, I bid thee, on the road,
And if it hap that midst of thy defeat,
Fainting beneath thy follies' heavy load,
My Master, GEOFFREY CHAUCER, thou do meet,
Then shalt thou win a space of rest full sweet;
Then be thou bold, and speak the words I say,
The idle singer of an empty day!

O Master, O thou great of heart and tongue,
Well mayst thou ask me why I wander here,
In raiment rent of stories oft besung!
But of thy gentleness draw thou anear,
And then the heart of one who held thee dear
Mayst thou behold! So near as that I lay
Unto the singer of an empty day.

.   .   .   .   .   .

Death have we hated, knowing not what it meant;
Life have we loved, through green leaf and through sere,
Though still the less we know of its intent:
The Earth and Heaven through countless year on year,
Slow changing, were to us but curtains fair,
Hung round about a little room where play
Weeping and laughter of man's empty day.

O Master, if thine heart could hear us yet,
Spite of things left undone, and wrongly done,
Some place in loving hearts then should we get,
For thou, sweet-souled, didst never stand alone,
But knew'st the joy and woe of many a one—
By lovers dead, who live through thee, we pray
Help thou us singers of an empty day!

7*

Few men lived days less "empty" than those of Morris, few men were less "idle" than he; yet in those words he was, whether consciously or not, describing an inner emptiness that springs from a secret doubt as to effort leading anywhere.

To study Morris's life is to be increasingly conscious of a strange alien quality in him. It is as though he had lived in the Fairy Hill and emerged into a world not his home. His curious remote eyes, which impressed even the friends who loved him most—was not their strangeness perhaps due to some quality in him that was not quite human? This quality is felt in much of his verse. This gave him power and great gifts, but it robbed him of humble happiness.

In the portrait Sir William Richmond painted of Morris this look can be seen—his face emerges from a swirl of hair like that of an ancient sea king appearing from the depths of the ocean, looking strangely at a strange world.

33

The last creative works of Morris's pen in the final years of his life were all of one kind—half a throwback to childhood, to the years gilded by nostalgic memory, half an escape into a world that never was. Out of the saga and the fairy-tale he created a new form of prose romance—a new and enchanting form, long and leisurely and beautifully told. "I must have a tale to tell", Morris said once in these last years. It is as though folk-history had been dipped in the waters of Lethe and the whole of existence wandered in a coloured dream. These differing stories, whatever their names, are all one endless tapestry which Morris wove with a curious ardour and patience, and which require an equal patience and ardour to read. They are good tales, things happen, there are finely imagined scenes finely described. The details are rich and full.

There is but one thing missing—none of the people have really any souls, in spite of mention of Holy Church and saints and rosary beads; and it is even doubtful if their hearts are anything but golden embroideries on a surcoat. In his actual tapestry designs Morris never did the faces and figures, they were always designed by Burne-Jones or others. In the same way he could not draw human beings in his romances; his people have names, they are young or old, beautiful or ugly, that is all. It is a changeling world, and after a while once the first enchantment has passed, no human can be quite happy there. Yet we cannot but suppose that Morris found some kind of happiness in this "Hollow Land" (his titles are suggestive) as he continued to go on writing these romances, these long romances of the strange lands where he was at home.

A Dream of John Ball does not belong to these stories, nor does *News From Nowhere*: they are in a different category. The first of them is *The House of the Wolfings*, followed by *The Roots of the Mountains*. These two have still links with human history, but in *The Story of the Glittering Plain* he has gone into his romance, saga-haunted world, and there he stayed while he wrote *The Well at the World's End*, *The Water of the Wondrous Isles*, and *The Sundering Flood*, which was the last he ever wrote.

Water was significant in Morris's life; it was part of his childhood homes, it belonged to his two last homes by the Thames, the two Kelmscotts; it was in the titles of these three last books he wrote.

Perhaps not many people in these hard and hurried days will have either the time or the temperament to appreciate the beauties of these books, for they have beauty in generous measure. They were written by a man who was near to the end of his days, but perhaps they will only continue to be read by the young, who still have time, and who, without much knowledge of sorrows, will find their faint melancholy (for melancholy underlies the gayest scenes) not unpleasing.

But these stories, though "fey" enough in many ways, have roots in the earth, because the man who wrote them had his roots there. And it was English earth (with a touch of Icelandic here and there) whatever names he gave it. His people might lack souls—his country did not. Both *The Well at the World's End* and *The Water of the Wondrous Isles* are full of the Wiltshire downland. That county had always appealed to him, from the days of his boyhood, and when those days were long past he wrote:

> The man must be hard to move indeed who is not moved as he turns the corner of one of our commonplace English highways and comes suddenly across that marvellous hedge of grey stones that our Saxon ancestors called Stonehenge: or looks from the great circular earthwork of Avebury—looks down on the little old village that lies within it, where the cottages are cheek by jowl with the few remaining stones of the ancient temple there: lying close by the huge barrow of Tilbury, the hills about all dotted with graves of the early chieftains; the mysterious Wandyke drawn across the downs at the back; wherein even now the horses are tethered when the yearly traditional horse-fair takes place at Tarn Hill. And lastly once more the Roman road running through it all towards Bath, just swerved a little by the huge mass of Silbury: a familiar place to my boyhood; yet a holy place indeed.

The defect of these long romances of Morris is perhaps not their defect but ours—they belong to an earlier and simpler time, as Morris essentially did himself. Told in the great hall of some medieval castle night after night, they would have received an enthralled attention; the adventures of Hallblithe and Golden Walter and Birdalone and all the others, the schemes of the wicked enchantress, would have provided talk for days. In this tired, sophisticated age the people seem little more than figures in a woven tapestry. Actually, we are more interested—unless, of course, we are very young, there could be no better tales for the long, long afternoons of youth—in the background, the "verdure" of these stories, at which Morris was such a

past master. The writing of them is simple and archaic to
just the right degree, and with that happy sense of being
at home in his half mythical, half historic past, which was
his peculiar gift. From his earliest days it was always said
of him that he did not read up things, he *knew*.

And what he knew and saw he could make others see.
Take this picture from *The House of the Wolfings*:

> There he was between the plough-stilts in the acres of the
> kindred when the west wind was blowing over the promise of
> early spring; or smiting down the ripe wheat in the hot after-
> noon amidst the laughter and merry talk of man and maid;
> or far away over Mirkwood Water watching the edges of the
> wood against the prowling wolf and lynx, the stars just begin-
> ning to shine over his head; or wending the windless woods
> in the first frosts before the snow came, the hunter's bow or
> javelin in hand; or coming back from the wood with the quarry
> on the sledge, across the snow, when winter was deep, through
> the biting icy wind and the whirl of the drifting snow, to the
> lights and music of the Great Roof, and the merry talk therein
> and the smiling of the faces glad to see the hunting-carles come
> back; and the full draughts of mead, and the sweet rest at night-
> tide when the north wind was moaning round the ancient
> home.

Or this, from *The Well at the World's End*:

> He looked at it all for a minute or two as the south-west wind
> went past his ears and played a strange tune on the innumerable
> stems of the bents and the hard-stalked blossoms, to which the
> bees sang counterpoint. Then the heart arose within him, and
> he drew his sword from the scabbard, and waved it about his
> head, and shook it toward the south and cried out, "Now,
> welcome world, and be thou blessed from one end to the other,
> from the ocean sea to the uttermost mountain!"

There are pages and pages of equally sharp and lovely
description in these romances—descriptions of the countryside, nearly always English under other names, though
sometimes the deserts and drear places are Icelandic;
descriptions of the beauty of buildings, of little cheaping

towns with a Cotswold flavour; of views and castles, and lovely ladies. Fairy, folk-tale, and Morris all mixed up together.

34

These romances were but a sideline, after all, in Morris's life. His activities in other ways still went on unceasingly. Even when he had more or less given up his socialist work he still lectured for them and for the Society for the Protection of Ancient Buildings; advised the authorities at the South Kensington Museum on the purchase of costly carpets and tapestries for the nation, and was concerned in the affairs of various arts and crafts societies and guilds, as well as his own business at Merton Abbey and the Oxford Street shop. There can have been few lives more filled to the brim than that of Morris.

But it was the thing he always wished.

"I tremble to think," he once said, "what would happen to me if I were forbidden my ordered daily work, and know that I should die of despair and weariness."

Towards the end of his life he declared gratefully: "This has been a jolly world to me, and I have always found plenty to do in it."

One of the things he always knew was not only the essential goodness of work, but that the man who alternates and varies his occupations was in little need of formal holidays. He had an instinctive wisdom of hand and head.

His socialism, though for years it took him away from the kind of work he loved best and could do best, was an attempt towards shaping a world in which human beings could live a simple and happy life, in homes where their sense of beauty and comfort would have room to grow, instead of being smothered under the ashes of ugliness and false values. In a letter written when he was a comparatively young man Morris had said (the letter has already been quoted) that a true civilization would be a much simpler one, in which people would live together in much smaller communities—the village idea, instead of the town idea—and having simplified life by having fewer wants and fewer possessions, would be able to look after themselves and find pleasure in doing it.

The "poet-upholsterer" was frequently reproached because the beautiful things he made were too costly for ordinary people to use in their homes. But what Morris preached was not luxury, but that the things of daily use should be comely and pleasant, though a degraded taste and bad economic conditions had made this rare in his time. There is no fundamental reason that comeliness should be costly, and in the kind of world he wanted that would not have been the case. The trouble was that for so long the manufacturers had taught the people to prefer a lot of poor things to the few good ones which might be bought for the same expenditure.

"I tell you", Morris once said,

I feel dazed at the thought of the immensity of work which is undergone for the making of needless things. It would be an instructive day's work for any one of us who is strong enough, to walk through two or three of the principal streets of London on a week-day, and take accurate note of everything in the shop-windows which is embarassing or superfluous to the daily life of a serious man. Nay, the most of these things no one, serious or unserious, wants at all; only a foolish habit makes even the lightest-minded of us suppose that he wants them, and to many people, even of those who buy them, they are obvious encumbrances to real work, thought, or pleasure.

In the Middle Ages people had fewer comforts but much more beauty, and that was the way that Morris would have had it. Of course we are bound to admit, with a smile, that Morris was very indifferent to comfort; he was too sturdy and violent to even notice its lack. When one of his customers complained that a chair he had made was not comfortable, Morris told him contemptuously that if he wanted comfort he could go to bed. But even in a bed Morris was content with wooden slats instead of springs; he thought embroidered hangings far more important than the quality of the mattress. If that should happen to be so bad as to destroy sleep, then Morris's remedy would be to get up and do a little weaving!

Another of his peculiarities was his dislike of mirrors; he would not have them in any of his houses or in his own bedroom—though it is probable that his wife and daughters must have secreted one or two somewhere for their own use. He declared:

> I have at least respect for the dwellers in the tub of Diogenes; indeed I don't look upon it as so bad a house after all. With a plane-tree and a clear brook near it, and some chance of daily bread and onions, it will do well enough.

This austerity is a little mitigated in the lecture on "The Lesser Arts of Life" from which the Diogenes quotation comes, when he says:

> . . . if we really care for art we shall not put up with something or other, but shall choose honest whitewash instead, on which sun and shadow play so pleasantly, if only our room be well planned and well shaped, and look kindly on us . . . if only our homes were built as they should be, we should want such a little furniture, and be so happy in that scantiness. . . . Simplicity is the one thing needful in furnishing, of that I am certain . . . our furniture should be good citizen's furniture, solid, and well-made in workmanship . . . it should be made of timber rather than walking-sticks.

A tender memory there of the "Incubi and Succubi" of his young Red Lion Square days.

There is a poem prefaced to *The House of the Wolfings* that also recalls memories of the Kentish home Morris never forgot:

> While in the early winter eve
> We pass amid the gathering night
> Some homestead that we had to leave
> Years past; and see its candles bright
> Shine in the room beside the door
> Where we were merry years agone
> But now must never enter more,
> As still the dark road drives us on,
> E'en so the world of men may turn
> At even of some hurried day
> And see the ancient glimmer burn
> Across the waste that hath no way;
> Then with that faint light in its eyes
> A while I bid it linger near
> And nurse its wavering memories,
> The bitter-sweet of days that were.

All of which shows that Morris was a man of roots, and that his roots were firmly fixed in his native soil. That cry from *News From Nowhere*, "O me! O me! How I love the earth and the seasons and the weather, and all things that deal with it, and all that grows out of it", is the cry of his own authentic voice, and is underneath all he does and thinks. But though he loved England so well in its rural aspects, he could be sharp enough on some of the other ones.

Once when he stayed at Rottingdean in the house on the Green Burne-Jones had bought—Rottingdean was only a tiny primitive village in those days—he went into Brighton to do some shopping and said ungallantly: "I think I saw more ugly people in Brighton in the course of an hour than I have seen otherwise for the last twenty years: as you justly remark, serves me right for going into Brighton."

But neighbouring Lewes met with kinder comment:

> We took a trap and drove to Lewes; you have to go a long way round, as the wheel-roads across the Downs are doubtful it seems: it is very beautiful when you get on to the brow of the hill above Falmer: a long way off to the right you can see Lewes

lying like a box of toys under a great amphitheatre of chalk hills: the whole ride is very pleasant: Lewes, when you get there lies on a ridge in its valley, the street winding down to the river (Ouse) which runs into the sea at Newhaven: on the whole it is set down better than any town I have seen in England.

The town itself he did not think equal to its position, but that was partly because there was a kink in Morris's nature which would not appreciate that charming High Street, with its delightful and largely unspoilt (this was in 1882) eighteenth-century and Regency houses with their bow-windows and dignified doorways.

His eye was acute, both for the things he disliked, as for those he liked intensely. However busy he might be at Merton Abbey, he could remember to write down:

There are some daffodils out already. The almond-tree is blossoming there beautifully; some of these fine days the place *has* looked pretty, the water sparkling among the twigs.

He filled pages of his letters to family and familiar friends about the growing things and the birds at Kelmscott. He knew a lot about birds, and watched them with care. He liked their aloof life, so untangled by human contacts. It was rather typical of him that he was an Englishman who was not a dog-lover; he was more inclined to care for a horse, and was certainly fond of the little Iceland pony who grew so fat and pampered at Kelmscott.

His observation of natural things is scattered throughout his poems, which are full of the loveliest descriptions of English scenes. One of his friends said that his hooded eyes seldom seemed to look at things or people, but all the time they had seen everything.

At the back of his crowded mind was even the fundamental idea of farming. He went to see a friend who had a smallholding, and thus described the experience:

I listened with longing heart to his account of his patch of ground, seven acres; he says that he and his fellow can almost live on it: they grow their own wheat and send flowers and fruit to Chesterfield and Sheffield markets: all that sounds very agreeable to me. It seems to me that the real way to enjoy life is to accept all its necessary ordinary details and turn them into pleasures by taking interest in them; whereas modern civilization huddles them out of the way, has them done in venal and slovenly manner till they become real drudgery, which people can't help trying to avoid. Whiles I think, as in a vision, of a decent community as a refuge from our mean squabbles and corrupt society; but I am too old now, even if it were not dastardly to desert.

35

In the course of his full and eager life there were few crafts at which Morris had not tried his hand, and against the commonly accepted idea that a Jack-of-all-trades is master of none, had proved himself a master of them all. The position he held in England and abroad as an artistic authority was entirely the fruit of his own efforts.

But one great craft and mystery he had not touched up to this time, and that was the trade of printing. He was too great a lover of the beauty of medieval work not to have been attracted by early illuminated books, and, as has been told, he developed a very fine script hand himself. But the printed book did not interest him particularly till near the end of his life. He owned books in considerable numbers, but was apt to treat them carelessly, and would fling volumes across the room if what the authors said annoyed him, or even out of the window. "It's only Master composing", said a servant to a visitor, whose arrival was greeted by a volume hurled out of a window. He was quite capable of leaving a book in a punt out all night in the rain. Ordinary books were not things of beauty, so unworthy of any special consideration.

Morris first became interested in the question of book production over book illustration. There was a project that Burne-Jones should do illustrations for the *Earthly Paradise*, which was to appear in a folio volume printed in double columns. Specimen pages were set up in Caslon type, and various kinds of paper tried, but it all came to nothing, and for many years Morris was concerned with other and, to him, more urgent matters.

Two things combined to turn Morris's mind in the direction of printing towards the end of his life. One was his desire to see his *The House of the Wolfings*, a book for which he had a special affection, as the writing of it had given him particular pleasure, printed in a more distinguished manner than the usual commercial style of that period, when printing was at a low ebb. The other thing that opened his eyes to the importance of good typography was that he had for friend and neighbour in Hammersmith— Emery Walker. Through the medium of the Chiswick Press the *Wolfings* book was given a satisfactory typographical dress, and the following year, in 1889, *The Roots of the Mountains* was produced in a manner even better.

"I am so pleased with my book," said the author, with the simplicity which never deserted him, "typography, binding, and must I say it, literary matter—that I am any day to be seen huggling it up, and am become a spectacle to Gods and men because of it."

When Morris said that he had only a bare seven more years to live. He was in his late fifties. He had done the work of at least four men in his lifetime and achieved not only an English but a European reputation. It hardly seemed likely that at so late an hour, when a little rest and leisure to enjoy the fruits of his labours would have appeared the natural thing, he should suddenly have taken up a completely new trade, and after a few years' work at it made a name for himself among the great printers of the world. Were everything else that he had done, were his poems and his chintzes alike wiped out, the name of William Morris would be remembered with honour as the creator of the Kelmscott Press. The Kelmscott *Chaucer*, the crown of that Press's work, is typographically one of the outstanding pieces of printing in the world, and will always remain so, however taste and ideas may change.

There is a saga quality about this story, and something of the saga simplicity in Morris's cry, when so late in his lifetime he discovered that glorious new craft: "I wish I had been a printer from my mother's womb."

36

Simple printer perhaps Morris never was. It was not in his Gothic nature to see type alone as sufficient to the printed page—or, rather, pages, for it is the twin pages of the opened book that the careful printer beholds, each complementary to the other, the two together in their spacing of type, leading, and margins making the completed unit. Morris's own printed page was adorned with ornament, borders, initial letters, even apart from illustration. Almost it seems that whatever he did he felt that Burne-Jones must have a part in it, be in the same boat—Ned could draw pictures, so pictures must come into Topsy's books. There are times when almost it might be wished that the Morris–Burne-Jones link had not been quite so strong, that Morris had stood entirely alone in his creative work. But it never was broken, though Morris's socialism clouded it for a time. After one of those regular Sunday morning breakfasts at The Grange, which were a feature of their friendship, Burne-Jones would retire to his studio and his dream world, while Morris set off to fight with beasts at Walham Green, never a word said on either side about the shadow between them. There cannot be much doubt as to which was the bigger man of the two.

But there was apparently no resentment in Morris's heart, even if he felt sore. He was not surprised if Burne-Jones shrank from his socialism, and he was unswervingly determined to have Ned with him when he could, so Burne-Jones had to come into the printing business with him to design decorations and pictures.

But the type face, after all, comes first in printing. An eye for it is not as common as it ought to be, but Morris had it by instinct, as he had so much else. In describing his aims in founding the Kelmscott Press, he said:

> I began printing books with the hope of producing some which would have a definite claim to beauty, while at the same time they should be easy to read and should not dazzle the eye or trouble the intellect of the reader by eccentricity of form in the letters . . . it was the essence of my undertaking to produce books which it would be a pleasure to look upon as pieces of printing and arrangement of type.

His unerring eye saw that it was not only the fount of type used that mattered in the final result, but the way it was used, the relation of word and line spacing to the type, and the type area in relation to the margins—which means how it is placed on the page. Each proportion is related to the other.

Morris, of course, would not have been the man he was had he not determined almost straightaway to design his own founts of type. He proceeded to do this with his usual inspired intrepidity, and, also in his usual manner, produced three noble founts, which are known as the Golden type, the Troy type, and the Chaucer type.

He describes in some detail how he came to design his Golden type. "What I wanted", he said,

> was letter pure in form; severe without needless excrescences; solid, without the thickening and thinning of the line which is the essential fault of the ordinary modern type, and which makes it difficult to read; and not compressed laterally, as all type has grown to be owing to commercial exigencies. There was only one source from which to take examples of this perfected Roman type, to wit, the works of the great Venetian printers of the fifteenth century, of whom Nicholas Jenson produced the completest and most Roman characters from 1470 to 1476.

He tells exactly how he worked with Jenson as his model:

> This type I studied with much care, getting it photographed to a big scale, and drawing it over many times before I began designing my own letter; so that though I think I mastered the essence of it I did not copy it servilely; in fact any Roman type, especially in the lower case, tends rather more to the Gothic than does Jenson's.

Having got his Golden Type, Morris inevitably wanted a Gothic, as well as a Roman fount, and so he designed the Troy type, in which he "strove to redeem the Gothic character from the charge of unreadableness, which is commonly brought against it".

When he was planning his great edition of Chaucer, the folio page printed in double column demanded a type of its own, and this Morris adapted from the one already cut and called after the book it was created for.

In one respect, little as he might have appreciated the comparison, Morris was like St. Paul, for he, too, could say: "This one thing I do, forgetting those things which are behind, and reaching forth unto those things which are before, I press towards the mark."

That a man should turn to the art of typography so late in life, and soar at once straight into the small company of the world's great printers, is a very remarkable achievement, and in and by itself probably the most notable of all the notable things that William Morris did. W. R. Lethaby, who understood what Morris was, said of him:

> ... when he did printing, he had to explore paper-making, ink-making, type-cutting, and other dozen branches of the trade. His ornaments and the treatment of Burne-Jones's illustrations were based on his personal practice as a wood-cutter. Morris was no mere 'designer' of type and ornament for books, but probably the most competent book-maker ever known. Indeed, it is a mistake to get into the habit of thinking of him as a 'designer'; he was a work-master—Morris the Maker!

Morris's own natural pleasure in his work is shown by two homely sayings. He once declared that all good designing is felt in the stomach, and on another occasion remarked: "I have an artichoke mind, no sooner do I pull off a leaf, than there's another waiting to be pulled."

The great Kelmscott edition of Chaucer was the crown of all his work. It was a tribute to his beloved master with whom he had walked gladly all his life. It is the noblest tribute that an English printer has ever paid to an English poet. Beautiful in our eyes, it would have been equally beautiful in Chaucer's—a fact which is itself remarkable. Such a triumph of printing was not achieved without the expenditure of much thought, and of time, of which precious commodity William Morris had but little left. He did but see his Chaucer completed when he had to leave it. For five years it was planned; for three years it was in preparation; the actual printing took all of two years save three months.

But naturally the infant Press did not start on such a vast undertaking as the Chaucer straight away. Morris's own *Story of the Glittering Plain* was the first book printed by the Kelmscott Press. Caxton's *Golden Legend*—for which the Golden type was designed by Morris—was the first important book printed. With his usual idea that the best was good enough, Morris—under heavy sureties—succeeded in borrowing from the Cambridge University Library the priceless copy of Caxton's own first edition of 1483, and it was from this edition that the Kelmscott Press volumes were set up.

It was at the beginning of 1891 that the Kelmscott Press actually started working in a cottage on Hammersmith Upper Mall, a stone's throw away from Kelmscott House. After a short time these premises proved too small, and larger premises were taken over next door at Sussex Cottage, which was really half of a large old family mansion called Sussex House. In the first home of the Kelmscott Press a proof-press and a printing-press were set up. The

A PAGE OF THE "KELMSCOTT CHAUCER."

staff was one compositor and one pressman—and Morris, who, of course, counted for a good deal more than one.

There is something enchantingly simple and right about it all. It fitted in so well with Morris's doctrine that "the true incentive to useful and happy labour is, and must be, pleasure in the work itself". And as the Press grew Morris imbued his workmen with much of his own spirit—as he worked side by side with them he had no need to preach Socialist doctrines to them. "To his own workmen", said Clutton-Brock, "he was masterful enough at times, but as their foreman and not as their social superior. He lost his temper with them sometimes, but always as man with man, and they recognized one of themselves when he did so."

Every detail of his new-discovered craft of printing was of absorbing interest to Morris. He even tried his hand at making the paper, and his second sheet was a very creditable example, though a beginner usually takes months before he can produce a decent sheet. But Morris's extraordinary fingers seemed at home in any pie.

But in the spring of this year in the very middle of his new joy in his Press, Morris was smitten down by a very severe attack of gout, accompanied by symptoms of serious kidney trouble. His doctors told him that he must henceforward consider himself a partial invalid and live with extreme care. But it was very difficult to make Morris into an invalid and he continued to regard work as the best cure for all human ills. He, so unlike Thomas Carlyle in most ways, yet would have echoed Carlyle's prayer: "Work to the end of my life, and life to the end of my work."

"It is a fine thing", said Morris, "to have some interesting work to do, and more than ever when one is in trouble —I found that out the other day."

But actually he had always known it.

Whether he was well or ill the work of the Kelmscott Press went forward—his driving spirit was always behind it whatever his tiresome body was doing. He never had much pity for Brother Ass.

37

The first two books printed by the Kelmscott Press were both Morris's own—*The Story of the Glittering Plain* and *Poems by the Way*. But Morris had not started the Press for the publishing of his own works; his ideas were far grander than that. *The Glittering Plain* was printed because there happened to be a small quantity of suitable paper just fitted for a small edition. In any case he would have regarded his own books as suitable to experiment upon while he was trying out ideas for greater works.

But in his *Poems by the Way* there is actually some of his loveliest and most tender work, and even in a study more of the man than of what he wrote, it is necessary to pause by the way over these poems, which here and there reveal more of his heart than he usually put on paper.

In this volume is that enchanting lyric "A Garden by the Sea" which many know—it had already seen the light in the fourth book of *The Life and Death of Jason*—who do not know that Morris wrote it.

> I know a little garden-close
> Set thick with lily and red rose,
> Where I would wander if I might
> From dewy morn to dewy night,
> And have one with me wandering.

Here are the charming little "Verses for Pictures" which show such aptness and delicacy of touch. Here is "Mine and Thine," the translation of an ancient Flemish poem which Morris has rendered so admirably:

> Yea, God well counselled for our health,
> Gave all this fleeting earthly wealth
> A common heritage to all,
> That men might feed them therewithal,
> And clothe their limbs and shoe their feet—
> And live a simple life and sweet.

But now so rageth greediness
That each desireth nothing less
Than all the world, and all his own;
And all for him and him alone.

And that was written in the fourteenth century, when
Morris was so apt to believe the world was nearer to what
he thought was good, the world he was striving after in
his socialism.

In these *Poems by the Way* there are examples of his
socialist verse—it can hardly be called poetry, except
perhaps for one unusual monologue, quite unlike Morris's
general work, called "Mother and Son", where the country-
bred working-class mother talks in the night to her baby
son of what has been, and what will be when he grows up
to fight the wrongs that oppress the poor.

A meditative piece, "The Half of Life Gone", is one of
Morris's admirable pastorals, wherein the country scenes
he has witnessed rise up before his brooding eyes, and
without strain or effort become "for ever England" on the
lovely page:

The days have slain the days, and the seasons have gone by
And brought me the summer again; and here on the grass I lie
As erst I lay and was glad ere I meddled with right and with
    wrong.
Wide lies the mead as of old, and the river is creeping along
By the side of the elm-clad bank that turns its weedy stream;
And grey o'er its hither lip the quivering rushes gleam,
There is work in the world as of old; they are eager at winning
    the hay,
While every sun sets bright and begets a fairer day.
The forks shine white in the sun round the yellow red-wheeled
    wain,
Where the mountain of hay grows fast; and now from out of the
    lane
Comes the ox-team drawing another, comes the bailiff and the
    beer,
And thump, thump, goes the farmer's nag o'er the narrow
    bridge of the weir.

Constable might have painted that scene: there are other pictures too:

> I will go adown by the water and over the ancient bridge,
> And wend in our footsteps of old till I come to the sunburnt ridge,
> And the great trench digged by the Romans; and thence awhile will I gaze,
> And see three teeming counties stretch out till they fade in the haze.

But the great treasure of *Poems by the Way* is Morris's "Message of the March Wind"—so lovely, so vital, with a freshness which time will not fade. One poem of this quality is enough to ensure a poet remembrance. Here his dream of a better world for which his man and maid are seeking, and for which they labour, is poetry, not propaganda, and the verses which record their joy sing in the heart:

> Fair now is the spring-tide, now earth is beholding
> With the eyes of a lover, the face of the sun;
> Long lasteth the daylight, and hope is enfolding
> The green-growing acres with increase begun.
>
> How sweet, sweet it is through the land to be straying
> 'Mid the birds and the blossoms and the beasts of the field;
> Love mingles with love and no evil is weighing
> On thy heart or mine, where all sorrow is healed.
>
> From township to township, o'er down and by tillage
> Far, far have we wandered and long was the day;
> But now cometh eve at the end of the village,
> Where over the grey wall the church riseth grey.
>
> There is wind in the twilight; in the white road before us
> The straw from the ox-yard is blowing about;
> The moon's rim is rising, a star glitters o'er us,
> And the vane on the spire-top is swinging in doubt.

Down there dips the highway, toward the bridge crossing
  over
The brook that runs on to the Thames and the sea,
Draw closer, my sweet, we are lover and lover;
This eve art thou given to gladness and me.

    .   .   .   .

But lo, the old inn, and the lights and the fire,
And the fiddler's old tune and the shuffling of feet;
Soon for us shall be quiet and rest and desire,
And to-morrow's uprising to deeds shall be sweet.

Things closely seen, and as closely felt, are in that poem.

38

In reading the works of Morris, both in prose and poetry,
the conviction is forced upon us that, fundamentally, he
did not alter. Up to a point this may be a source of
strength—a man who knows what he wants, who is all
of a piece, is certain to accomplish something. But it is also
a weakness in that it implies lack of growth, and growth
and change are a necessary part of life.

Morris's mental landscape is beautiful, but it is monotonous. Fair meadows spread around, rich with enamelled
flowers, a stream meanders gently by, a noble stone barn
rises like a church, and dwellings grey-roofed, or maybe
"thatched with gold", cluster close by, surrounded by
little orchards where rosy apples always hang amid the
lichened boughs. Amidst this pleasant pastoral scene rises
a stark and stony peak, grim and forbidding, with lightning
flashing among its heights. In this rather curious landscape Morris is quite at home, and many people may take
pleasure in it for a while, but after a time they wander
away—there is something missing, though it is a little
difficult to say what.

And though Morris was Lord of the Manor of all this

fair demesne, and made it and enjoyed it, perhaps he, too, found something missing. One thing at least is clear in his life—he was always questing for something, and it is equally clear he never found it. At no time of his life is the expression of his much-photographed face that of a contented man. His boisterous high spirits, his Topsyness, his violence and temper and strong language, are like a barrier he erected against silence. His need to be making and doing was partly, it may be guessed, to prevent thinking. This was something of a changeling world, where the human values had gone astray. All the people in his prose tales are not really human, they do not act or think or speak like human beings— or only on the surface. There is nothing under the skin of human blood. No human being could live in such a world as depicted in *News from Nowhere* with its charming young men and maidens, without going mad. And there is one odd and significant thing about this world as Morris planned it—there are no old women, no "knitters in the sun", in the autumnal sun of their ageing lives.

Morris read and delighted in Dickens, and appreciated the rough and unusual in character, yet there is no touch of these qualities in his stories. His world is peopled by the young, the vigorous, the beautiful, with a few grave old kings and counsellors here and there. They are all without either brains, character, or any qualities to make them real and lovable. If they are bad they are black, if they are good they are white, but there is no essential difference. His characters are really the people of folk-tales, yet lacking in their sharp outlines and homely humour, lacking the fundamental simplicity and earthiness of the folk-tale. Morris, however hard he tried to go backwards in time, was yet a modern, and deeply touched with the modern sense of a troubled world. He was utterly unable, as the makers of the early stories were able, and as was his master Chaucer, to see their salvation in a Child, born of a Maiden "that was makeless".

Knowing how unhappy most people would be condemned to live in this story world of Morris, even if age
were permitted entry there, is it cause for wonder that
Morris, growing old—for his very strenuous life had aged
him somewhat too soon—was himself not happy?

Across this "Sundering Flood," and out of these "Woods
beyond the World", Morris came at the end of his life to
lay eager, almost desperate hands upon the concrete and
glorious task of printing a noble edition of his beloved
Chaucer's *Canterbury Tales*. It was something he could do
about which he had no doubts, it was something he could
leave behind him to future generations—as those fore-
runners of his whose work he loved to adoration had left
their painted books, their illuminated parchments, and
their carven stones.

39

Before the great ship the *Chaucer* was set up on the stocks,
a whole fleet of smaller vessels had been launched from the
Kelmscott Press beside the flowing Thames. It is not
needful to enumerate all their names, which may be found
in Halliday Sparling's admirable book on the Kelmscott
Press. Into their fine quality and high standard of printing
Morris threw all his still abounding enthusiasm. In this
work he owed much to his friends and colleagues, Emery
Walker and Sidney Cockerell. He had reached the stage
when he could no longer carry the full burden on his own
shoulders.

But one thing he did entirely on his own—with a few
slight exceptions—was to design not only all the type, but
the borders, the title-pages, and ornaments used by the
Kelmscott Press for all the books bearing its imprint. He
had the art of combining weight with delicacy—flimsy
ornament was abhorrent to his Gothic soul—in his borders

and title-pages, and this gives its own peculiar quality and distinction to the Kelmscott Press books. When he had finished the ornament for the first page of the Chaucer to his satisfaction, he exclaimed simply: "My eyes! how good it is!"

The last years of Morris's life were woven, as it were, round his Chaucer. As was to be expected in so large an undertaking, there were delays and difficulties, all of which in his pressing anxiety to see the great work completed— he knew quite well that his days were ending—he found very hard to bear. Even for a moment, because of this, he let go his clutch upon the utmost attainable perfection. When somebody looking at Burne-Jones's designs for the illustrations, suggested that the second set were better than the first, Morris angrily forbade him to say this to the artist, for fear Burne-Jones should want to do them all over again. He was acutely depressed when some of the ink was imperfectly mixed and was found to stain the page—though fortunately it was found possible to bleach it out, so this did not cause a great delay. He made a design for the binding, but was forced to say: "Leather is not good now, what used to take nine months to cure is done in three. They used to say, what's longest in the tan-yard stays least time in the market: but that no longer holds good. People don't know how to buy now, they'll take anything."

The nearer the Chaucer grew to completion the more agitated and anxious Morris became. He could not wait. He cried when asked what date would satisfy him for publication: "I'd like it finished to-morrow; every day beyond to-morrow that it isn't done is one too many." The Easter holidays of his last year of life, 1896, were almost more than he could bear in his weakness and im-patience—"Four mouldy Sundays in a mouldy row, the press shut and Chaucer at a standstill."

But on the second day of June the first two completed copies of the great Chaucer came from the binders—one for Morris, and one for Burne-Jones. For five years that magnificent edition had been planned. Burne-Jones adorned it with eighty-seven illustrations, and all the borders, initial letters large and small, and the woodcut title-page were designed by Morris. The white pigskin binding with silver clasps was also his design. Neither time, nor money, nor love, had been grudged by him to his noble Chaucer.

When the completed folio was delivered to his hands at Kelmscott House in Hammersmith on the second of June 1896 Morris had exactly four months more to live.

40

To follow the great Chaucer through to its completion is to come very close to the completion of Morris's own life. So it becomes necessary to go back a little way and pick up some dropped threads that must be knotted in to the fabric of his existence.

Morris was not what could be truly called a bookish man, in spite of his own very considerable output in prose and poetry, in which he had attained such eminence that after Tennyson's death he was approached as to whether he would consider the Laureateship were it offered to him. As might be expected from his good sense, Morris declined. He could not in any way imagine himself writing official odes, much as he enjoyed composing his own kind of poetry. In fact he enjoyed writing his own tales more than reading other men's, with a few exceptions, and got the same sense of relaxation from writing that most people do from the more indolent reading. Even when weak and ill he would rise from his bed to refresh himself by writing a few pages of his last romance, with its pathetically appropriate title of *The Sundering Flood*.

His memory was so good that he did not need, once he

had read a book, to read it again—he knew it, or if it was no use to him, forgot it. He was not a scholar, or one of those people who would almost prefer to read books about books rather than the books themselves. Such proceedings filled his direct mind with scorn. There was no "critical apparatus" about his Chaucer—there was just Chaucer. When Burne-Jones gave his own magnificent copy to his daughter Margaret, he pointed this out. "I want particularly to draw your attention", he said, " to the fact that there is no preface to Chaucer, and no introduction, and no essay on his position as a poet, and no notes, and no glossary; so that all is prepared for you to enjoy him thoroughly."

Except for desultory reading—though that was fairly extensive—and for his own works, Morris in his youth and maturity was not a notable bookman. His life was far too full of other things—architecture, the domestic crafts, learning languages, travel, socialism and all it led to. Then suddenly, as it seemed, in his last years he discovered books—books that is as a passion. He became a printer. His beauty-loving eyes turned on the printed page— hitherto he had only seen the written page in this light; calligraphy, not printing, had attracted him—as one of man's major works. He not only decided to produce fine printing himself but he began passionately to collect *incunabula*, to study the work of notable presses of the early days of printing.

He had never cared about money, having been born to a sufficiency of it, and he had always used it with easy generosity and freedom. But there was beneath this apparent carelessness a good middle-class common sense on the matter of money—he spent it, but he did not recklessly fling it about. However, when his last passion for *incunabula*, and still more for painted books, came upon him, he did not hesitate to spend hundreds of pounds for a volume he desired, without which he had decided that life was not worth living.

(Photo: Emery Walker Ltd.)

KELMSCOTT HOUSE: THE LIBRARY.

Owing to his own knowledge—a thing that seemed innate in him whenever he was interested in any subject —and the valuable advice of friends like F. S. Ellis and Sidney Cockerell, he quite soon acquired a remarkable collection of manuscripts and early printed books. "The first printed books were the best ever done," said Morris, "the first and the last of fine printing." This was the final joy life offered him, and it came in the right shape for a man who had lived so hard and used up his bodily energies so ruthlessly that at a comparatively early age he was obliged to economize his strength. But to sit at home and study beautiful books with an acute rejoicing eye, to be wealthy enough to send people to Paris and Germany to buy books for his collection, does not need robust health. And Morris enjoyed to the full the excitement and happiness of his new pursuit. He was coming to the end of his days, but not to the end of his enthusiasms, so in the true sense he never grew old. His sight was the most precious of all his senses to him; through his eyes he saw life. His sense of hearing was much less vital to him, and only now and then, especially in his last days, was he truly touched by music.

He wrote something on this matter of seeing which explains him a good deal:

Perhaps mankind will regain their eyesight, which they have lost to a great extent; people have largely ceased to take in mental impressions through the eyes, whereas in times past, the eyes were the great feeders of the fancy and imagination. I am in the habit when I go to an exhibition or a picture gallery of noticing their behaviour there; and as a rule I note that they seem very much bored, and their eyes wander vacantly over the various objects exhibited to them. If ordinary people go to our National Gallery, the thing which they want to see is the Blenheim Raphael, which, though well done, is a very dull picture to anyone not an artist. While, when Holbein shows them the Danish princess of the sixteenth century yet living on the canvas, the demure half-smile not yet faded from her eyes;

when Van Eyck opens a window for them into Bruges of the fourteenth century; when Botticelli shows them Heaven as it lived in the hearts of men before theology was dead, these things produce no impression on them, not so much even as to stimulate their curiosity and make them ask what 'tis all about; because these things were done to be looked at, and to make the eyes tell the mind tales of the past, the present, and the future.

Tales of the past were what his eyes were always telling Morris, and he found them perhaps most vividly in painted books, with the early printed ones which were his last loves. He did not much care for hanging pictures on his walls, and considering his life spent among artists he possessed very few. After his Oxford years he rarely bought a picture, but he was willing to spend hundreds of pounds on a single book.

He gave nearly £400 for an English Book of Hours, written in East Anglia, about 1300. Two leaves were missing from this book, which were afterwards discovered to be in the Fitzwilliam Museum at Cambridge. This was an agonizing state of affairs not to be endured, and after long negotiations it was agreed that the Fitzwilliam Museum should let Morris have the two leaves to insert into and complete his Book of Hours, on consideration that he sold his Book of Hours to the Museum for £200 and that it was to go there after his death. The Museum was very much the gainer by this arrangement, as Morris only lived to enjoy the treasure for something over a year.

On a lower scale he bought: "for £15 10s. (much too dear) a Guldin Bibel Augsburg, Hohenwang, *circa* 1470; a very interesting book which I much wanted. Also I bought for £25 (much too dear) a handsome 13th-century French MS., but with little ornament, because it looked so handsome I hadn't the heart to send it back."

He went to another sale where he did not succeed in buying anything. "Two books I bid for," he says:

a 13th-century Aristotelian book with three very pretty initials, but imperfect top and tail; I put £15 on this with many misgivings as to my folly—hi! it fetched £50!! A really pretty little book, Gregory's Decretals, with four or five very tiny illuminations; I took a fancy to it and put £40 on it, expecting to get it for £25—ho!! it fetched £96!!! Rejoice with me that I have got 82 MSS, as clearly I shall never get another.

But he did, two very wonderful ones—the Huntingfield Psalter, a magnificent end of the twelfth century-example, and a missal, the Tiptoft Missal, early fourteenth-century work, with marvellous illuminated borders. He had also the Speculum Humanae Salvationis of 1483, with all its original woodcuts. The best thing he bought was the wonderful Windmill Psalter, for which he gave £1,000.

And amid such rare and noble treasures as these Morris's own Kelmscott Chaucer was worthy to take its place. As William Gaunt says in his *Pre-Raphaelite Tragedy:*

> Morris had not produced a book for the age in which he lived. He had produced a book for the age in which he did not live. Its luminous pages existed in a void which remained to be fitted by the ideal society of which he had dreamed, towards which he yearned with a longing never to be fulfilled.

Morris probably knew this, but as he once said in one of his lectures: "To know that men lived and worked mightily before you is an incentive for you to work faithfully now, that you may leave something to those who come after you."

41

But though after he became a printer, the printed book, as well as painted psalters and missals, meant so much to him, Morris did not cease to care for other things. Architecture had been his first love, and in the penultimate years of his life he was still working for that cause, particularly in the service of Peterborough Cathedral, threatened by the "Restorers". Morris had known and loved this great fabric in his boyhood; it was fitting he should set his lance in rest in its defence when he was sixty-two. Many years earlier he had described it in the *Earthly Paradise*, in the Introduction to the story of "The Proud King":

> I who have seen
> So many lands, and midst such marvels been,
> Clearer than these abodes of outlaw men
> Can see above the green and unburnt fen
> The little houses of an English town,
> Cross-timbered, thatched with fen-reeds coarse and
> brown,
> And high o'er these, three gables, great and fair,
> That slender rods of columns do upbear
> Over the minster doors, and imagery
> Of kings, and flowers no summer field doth see,
> Wrought on those gables. Yea, I heard withal
> In the fresh morning air, the trowels and all
> Upon the stone, a thin noise far away;
> For high up wrought the masons on that day,
> Since to the monks that house seemed scarcely well
> Till they had set a spire or pinnacle
> Each side the great porch.

In the same year Morris made another journey for the same object, the Society for the Protection of Ancient Buildings, and in the same eastern quarter of England, to Suffolk. "A pretty journey", he said:

all through my native Essex. The upland pastures were all burnt up, and were cocoanut matting; but the corn did not look bad: they were cutting oats in many places, which should not be ready till the end of August. Blyborough was what we went to see; once a good town in the Middle Ages, now a poor remnant of a village with the ruins of a small religious house and a huge fifteenth-century church, built of flints after that country manner: a very beautiful church, full of interest, with

fine woodwork galore, a lovely painted roof, and some stained
glass; the restorations not much noticeable from the inside:
floor of various bricks, a few seats in the nave, all ancient,
similar ones in the chancel, and the rest open space. We were
cumbered of course with the parson, since we came to advise
him, but I much enjoyed myself. . . . The place is close to
Southwold on the little tidal river Bly at the end of the marsh-
land valley, where they were busy with their second hay crop.
Little spits of the sandy low upland covered with heather and
bracken run down to the marsh, and make a strange landscape
of it; a mournful place, but full of character. I was there some
twenty-five years ago; and found I remembered it perfectly.

It will be seen that William Morris was faithful in his
loves, and that in his case there was no doubt of the child
being father of the man. But in a very particular sense
Kelmscott Manor had become the home of his heart, and
his last years are all embroidered at the edges with accounts
of snatched visits there, of the flowers growing in the garden
at the different seasons, of the birds singing there. He had
been very proud of Kelmscott's modest topiary work, and
had liked to clip the dragons and peacocks himself, but
he began to find the job too exhausting, little as he was
inclined to yield to his doctor's orders as to leading a
quiet life. But he could still walk about the gardens and
orchard and the farm adjoining, and observe the tall
hollyhocks which were a feature of the Kelmscott borders,
and look on the flowing Thames.

42

It was his great edition of Chaucer which kept Morris
keyed up to the end of his days. It was his final work, and
completed in full perfection. It is that which must be
remembered; not the increasing weakness, the failing of
the powers of that vigorous body, driven too hard by the

eager, ever-questing mind. His doctor said that the disease
he died of was "simply being William Morris, and having
done more work than most ten men". Even his remedies
for illness were of an heroic nature. He made a last futile
voyage to Iceland, thinking the sight of the beloved land
might help him, and that there he might come on the
health which he was not to find again in this world. He
kept going so long as he could keep going, and no man
can do more. Nearly a couple of years before his death his
robust common sense fitly rebuked a friend who would
pretend to him that his increasing weakness was due to
January being the worst time of the year. "No, it ain't",
said Morris bluntly. "It's a very fine time of year indeed:
I'm getting old, that's what it is."

There was little subtlety and no nonsense about Morris.
It showed in his writings. As Burne-Jones said wisely:

> Chaucer is very much the same sort of person as Morris;
> unless he can begin his tale at the beginning and go on steadily
> to the end, he's bothered. There is no ingenuity in either of
> them; the value of their work comes from the extreme simplicity
> and beautiful directness of their natures.

As was his writing, so was his reading. He liked a tale
where things happened and men arrived somewhere. All
the simple great stories of the world were after his own
heart, as he has shown so superbly in his *Earthly Paradise*.
When he was reading for his own private pleasure he
read those kind of tales, not explorations into the personal
complexes and the inhibitions of hero and heroine, nor
novels based on the comedy of the social scene. The only
thing that came out of America for which he cared was
Huckleberry Finn, which he loved, and used to read almost
with uproarious enjoyment.

His favourite authors were Scott, Dickens, and Surtees,
Cobbett and Borrow—all startlingly British, it will be seen,
though for Dumas he also had a taste. He was not a great
Shakespearian, partly because the drama did not appeal

to him. He liked Keats better than Shelley—as he said Shelley had "no eyes". But Blake delighted him—"the part of him which a mortal can understand"—as Blake, among many other things, was forthright and a hard hitter. Milton he had no use for. "I hope I shall escape boycotting at the hands of my countrymen for leaving out Milton," Morris said, "but the union in his works of cold classicalism with Puritanism (the two things which I hate most in the world) repels me so that I *cannot* read him."

He admired old bludgeoning Thomas Carlyle, and according to his daughter May found *Frederick the Great* a humorous work. Its alarming length would certainly not deter him, for he was one of those gifted readers who can almost take in a page at a single glance—yet he had a truly marvellous memory for all he read; a book once read was his for life. When he was in the mood for reading it was difficult to keep him supplied, his appetite and capacity was so enormous. On one occasion he declared that having "done Mommsen" he had nothing to read, and would, if somebody did not come to his assistance, be reduced to reading cookery books or his own works. Gibbon's *Decline and Fall* was a mere snack by the way. Doughty's *Arabia Deserta* was a constant joy to him. But, as might be expected, when someone thrust Barrie's newly published *Little Minister* into his hands he dropped it promptly after one look. "I don't belong to the parish", he said briefly. He called Montaigne "One of the Seven Humbugs of Christendom".

In his reading, as in other things, Morris had the sense and strength of mind to hold on to the things he liked, the things that naturally belonged to him, and let the others go. It may be narrow, but it is deep digging produces the best fruits.

It is characteristic of his natural energy that he loved reading aloud—which he did very well, if he was not reading his own works, to which he never did proper justice—but much disliked being read to. His daughter describes the wonderful evenings he used to give them round the hearth in the Tapestry Room at Kelmscott, reading Dickens or Huck Finn, or the *Arabian Nights* to them, making everything so vivid and alive. But if anyone read aloud to him he became restless, or said he did not care for the book. This was a trial when he was ill and was too tired to read to himself, and yet could not bear to be read to, much as he wanted that consolation.

At the very end of his life Morris touched the fringe of an art which had meant but little to him. Till then he had preferred to look at an early painting of an angel playing a lute or the virginals, to listening to somebody less than an angel playing that lute or the virginals. Music had been to him not much more than "noises off" in his crowded and active life.

But when his life became perforce so much less active, music, the Heavenly Maid, stepped softly over his threshold for a brief farewell moment. Not modern music, not Romantic music, even in its noblest form, still less turgid Wagnerian music for which Morris had such a hearty loathing, but music in a pure and lovely guise—early English music. And the conditions were as nearly possible perfect—for to Kelmscott House looking on the Thames, which Morris had made so beautiful inside with the works of his own hands, where his precious painted books, his *incunabula*, his own great Chaucer bound in pigskin and silver-clasped, were stored, Arnold Dolmetsch brought a pair of virginals and played the music of William Byrd to William Morris.

The musician said of his listener:

> He had for long deplored the fact that, amongst all the Arts, music alone had no attraction for him. He could find no pleasure in piano recitals and big orchestras; but, when he heard the kind of music whose ideals and purposes correspond with the arts he loved, he was profoundly moved. He was ever grateful to me for having filled in his all-embracing mind the place that music alone could fill.

When on this last occasion Dolmetsch, so perfect an
artist, played a pavan and galliard of Byrd's to Morris:
"He broke into a cry of joy", says his biographer, "at the
opening phrases, and after the two pieces had been repeated at his request, was so deeply stirred that he could
not bear to hear any more."

43

When Morris was at Kelmscott Manor he slept in a
great Elizabethan four-post bed, in his Elizabethan bed-
chamber, which everyone had to walk through in the
true Elizabethan manner if they wanted to go to the
Tapestry Room. This massive bed—evidently built by
some long-past carpenter to stand up to Morris's ways with
furniture—was richly curtained in embroideries worked by
his daughter May. She had embroidered all round the
canopy frill the verses he wrote for that bed at Kelmscott,
punctuating the lines with little birds and leaves and
flowers—a very beautiful piece of needlework.

> The wind's on the wold
> And the night is a-cold,
> And Thames runs chill
> 'Twixt mead and hill.
> But kind and dear
> Is the old house here
> And my heart is warm
> 'Midst winter's harm.
> Rest then and rest,
> And think of the best
> 'Twixt summer and spring,
> When all birds sing
> In the town of the tree,
> And ye lie in me
> And scarce dare move
> Lest earth and its love

Should fade away
Ere the full of the day.
I am old and have seen
Many things that have been;
Both grief and peace
And wane and increase.
No tale I tell
Of ill or well,
But this I say,
Night treadeth on day,
And for worst and best
Right good is rest.

But the time was come when whatever bed he lay in and however still he lay, "earth and its love" would fade away from him. His early obsession with the idea of death had largely left him, and he could say with a certain detachment:

As for death, I find that, never having experienced it, I have no conception of what it means, and so cannot even bring my mind to bear upon it. I know what it is to live; I cannot even guess what it is to be dead.

He could not say *Spero* because he was unhappily unable to say *Credo*.

44

Morris did not die in his beautiful old bed—he did not die in his beloved Kelmscott under that grey-gabled roof, among the trees then shedding their leaves, and the fading flowers of the late autumn garden. He died in Hammersmith on a Saturday morning, the 3rd of October 1896.

Saturday morning in Hammersmith in those days, fifty years ago, was full of a homely shabby busy-ness—the housewives engaged in shopping pushing slowly along the pavement, anxious to miss no bargains; the butchers standing at their open doorways shouting the merits of

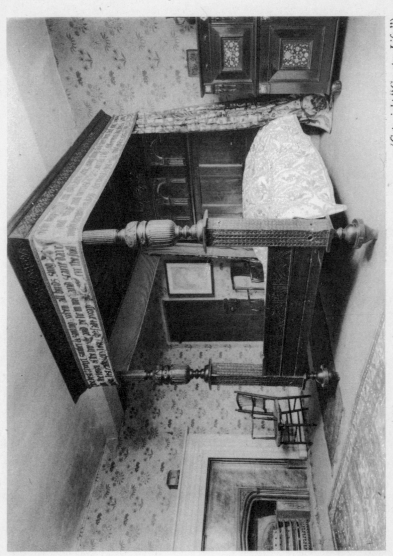

KELMSCOTT MANOR: MORRIS'S BEDROOM

their great slabs of meat, while the purchasers pinched the steaks in a determined effort to get good value for their scanty cash; the hoarse vendors of apples and bunches of Michaelmas daisies shuffling their barrows along the kerbs of narrow and unbeautiful King Street; the horse-buses trying to avoid them and all the people walking in the roadway. And standing at street corners, or leaning against pub walls, lounging down-at-heel men, with their hands in their empty pockets, caps pulled over their eyes—eyes in which there was no hope of happiness, except such happiness as a pint of beer can bring.

And only a little retreated from all this shabby busy scene was the little quiet backwater by the river, where in the plain old Georgian house, in an oasis of garden set with tall trees, Morris was dying. Before his windows flowed the Thames, ruffled and shining in the October breeze— the Thames whose waters had come down past that Manor House at Kelmscott he would see no more.

Morris died at Hammersmith, but he was buried as was fitting in the little churchyard at Kelmscott.

There was an undertaker at Hammersmith who advertised the solemn fact that he "conducted Funerals with Respectability and Economy. Stud of 27 Black Horses kept." But none of the 27 black horses waited before the door of Kelmscott House on the Upper Mall, with their black plumes tossing in the river breeze, for the coffin of William Morris. It was much simpler and happier than that. His body was carried to the grave by one of the Kelmscott farm wagons, painted in the traditional gay yellow, with big red wheels, and the horse that drew it was led by one of the Kelmscott farm carters. It might have been the burial centuries earlier of that William Morys, farmer, whom his later namesake liked to remember. The day of the funeral, Tuesday the 6th of October, was wet and wild and stormy. A south-westerly gale was tearing through the sky, and the floods were out round about, and all the little streams singing with a loud voice.

Morris would have loved it. His childish liking for water had always stayed with him.

That old friend Philip Webb, who had designed and built William Morris's first home of his own, the Red House, made a little stone roof for his last one. It was very simple, with nothing cut on it but the name and the two dates, 1834–1896, and four little oak leaves. A bay-tree was planted at the head, and at the foot thorn and box.

William Morris lived an infinitely fuller and richer life than falls to the lot of any but a few men. He had a certain quality of genius and used it finely. The outward circumstances of his life were kind. But underneath all that he did and achieved and was, it is impossible not to feel a deep sense of frustration. It was the Changeling in him— that *berserk* temper of his is one of the signs of the Changeling, the child who does not belong here. He was always struggling with a world in which he was not properly at home. He was not really happy—that was why he was always looking for happiness in different forms of work, expecting to find it in the dye-vat, or the loom, or the composing-stick. No more than the Changeling could he find the happiness he sought in human love. Under all his kindness and affection and generosity it is quite evident that he did not really know much about it. "He doesn't want anybody", said the friend who was closest to him throughout his life. "He lives absolutely without the need of man or woman."

Even in the matter of manners—which after all are the means of contact between ordinary human beings—there was something strange about Morris. He did not in the least realize his effect upon people. He regarded himself as a very polite person: "prided himself upon his manners", said his biographer, "and was capable of the most annoying and almost supernatural rudeness towards both men and women."

As if he were a stranger in a strange land, who did not know the customs of the country.

There was surely a kinship between him and that wonderful seventeenth-century Tom O'Bedlam:

> With a heart of furious fancies,
>   Whereof I am Commander:
>   With a burning spear
>   And a horse of air,
>   To the wilderness I wander;
> With a Knight of ghosts and shadows,
>   I summoned am to Tourney:
>   Ten leagues beyond
>   The wide world's end;
>   Methinks it is no journey.

To Morris, the world as he saw it about him at the close of the nineteenth century had a Bedlam air—everyone seemed to him, save for a few here and there, to be rushing in anxious pursuit of filthy shadows, leaving behind them the beauty which, to him, was the principal meaning of existence. Amidst this mad scene Morris had been seeking for his real home. He never found it. He died too young, with his work incomplete, but perhaps his heart, under its armour of aloofness, was broken. There is no reason for living then.

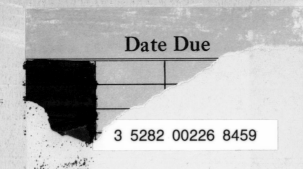